Favorite Prayers
to Our Lady

Mary was the Mother of Jesus and His Associate in the Work of Redemption. By devout and assiduous prayer to her we can go "to Jesus through Mary."

FAVORITE PRAYERS TO OUR LADY

The Most Beautiful Prayers found in
the Liturgy and Tradition of the Church,
including the Writings of Saints and Popes,
and the Faithful Devoted to Mary

By

Anthony M. Buono

Editor of the Dictionary of Mary

Illustrated

CATHOLIC BOOK PUBLISHING CORP.
New Jersey

NIHIL OBSTAT: James T. O'Connor, S.T.D.
Censor Librorum

IMPRIMATUR: ✠ Patrick J. Sheridan, D.D.
Vicar General, Archdiocese of New York

The Nihil Obstat and Imprimatur are official declarations that a book or a pamphlet is free of doctrinal or moral error. No implication is contained therein that those who have granted the Nihil Obstat and Imprimatur agree with the contents, opinions or statements expressed.

(T-919)

CONTENTS

FOREWORD

Prior to the Second Vatican Council (which was held from 1962 to 1965), Catholics had a strong devotion to Mary, the Mother of God. After the Council, there was a temporary decrease in that devotion. Then devotion to Mary returned stronger than ever.

The reason for this renewed increase in Marian devotion is not hard to find—the Church has always possessed and preached true devotion to Mary, the Mother of Jesus, and the wonderful spiritual results that flow from it. A strong proponent of this teaching was Pope John Paul II, who wrote among other things:

"For every Christian and for every human being, Mary is the one who first 'believed,' and precisely with her faith as Spouse and Mother she wishes to act upon all those who entrust themselves to her as her children.

"And it is well known that the more her children persevere and progress in this attitude the nearer Mary leads them to the 'unsearchable riches of Christ' (Eph 3:8).

"And to the same degree they recognize more and more clearly the dignity of the human being in all its fullness and the definitive meaning of the human vocation" (*The Mother of the Redeemer,* no. 46).

Today, there is more interest in Mary than ever. Marian books of prayer and devotion proliferate on all sides. People want to read about Mary, show their love for Mary, and pray to Mary.

The present book is intended to fill the need of those who wish to pray to our Lady in *accord with the mind of the Church.* It contains both traditional and contemporary prayers to our Lady that can be used for all occasions.

Some of the prayers are taken from the Church's Liturgy, others from the Church's living Tradition, including the wide repertory of prayers composed by Saints and holy Popes, and still others from the life-situation of Catholics throughout the ages.

Hence, this book constitutes a short compendium of approved prayers to Mary that can be used at a moment's notice. At the same time, it can act as a pattern for personal prayers that the readers can compose for themselves.

Every effort has been made to insure that this book will be easy to use and attractive to those praying. The text is printed in large pleasing typeface and in red and black. The inspiring illustrations of Mary, with or without her Son, will help keep our minds on Jesus and through Him on the other Persons of the Blessed Trinity.

May all who use this prayerbook achieve a deeper and more vital spiritual life. May it lead them through Mary ever closer to the eternal union with the living God.

PRAYING TO MARY IS OUR CHRISTIAN HERITAGE
—From the beginning Christians have praised Mary
as the Mother of God and prayed to her both in the
Liturgy and in private prayer. She is "the glory of
[the heavenly] Jerusalem, . . . the surpassing pride
of [the new] Israel, . . . the great honor of our
[Christian] people" (Judith 15:9).

POPULAR MARIAN PRAYERS

In a magnificent Apostolic Exhortation of February 2, 1974, Pope Paul VI set down the basis for prayer to Mary:

"The Church's norm of faith requires that her norm of prayer should everywhere blossom forth with regard to the Mother of Christ. Such devotion to the Blessed Virgin is firmly rooted in the revealed Word and has solid dogmatic foundations. It is based on the singular dignity of Mary, Mother of the Son of God, and therefore beloved Daughter of the Father and Temple of the Holy Spirit— Mary, who, because of this extraordinary grace, is far greater than any other creature on earth or in heaven" (Devotion to the Blessed Virgin Mary, *no. 56*).

The Bishops of the United States gave further details in a splendid Pastoral Letter of November 21, 1973:

"When Mary is honored, her Son is duly acknowledged, loved, and glorified, and His commandments are observed. To venerate Mary correctly means to acknowledge her Son, for she is the Mother of God. To love her means to love Jesus, for she is always the Mother of Jesus.

"To pray to our Lady means not to substitute her for Christ, but to glorify her Son Who desires us to have loving confidence in His Saints, especially in His Mother. To imitate the 'faithful Virgin' means to keep her Son's commandments" (Behold Your Mother, no. 82).

The prayers in this section, like those in the rest of the book, are intended to help us pray to Mary in the way the Church wants: in line with the Bible, in harmony with the Liturgy, in an ecumenical spirit, and in accord with the latest anthropological studies. (See Paul VI, Devotion . . . , nos. 29-39.)

Traditional Prayers

Hail Mary
(Ave Maria)

Hail Mary,
full of grace,
the Lord is with you.
Blessed are you among women
and blessed is the fruit of your womb,
Jesus.

Holy Mary,
Mother of God,
pray for us sinners,
now and at the hour of our death.

We Fly to Your Patronage
(Sub Tuum)

We fly to your patronage,
O holy Mother of God;
despise not our petitions
in our necessities,
but deliver us always from all dangers,
O glorious and blessed Virgin.

Mary, Mother of Grace

Mary, Mother of grace,
Mother of mercy,
shield me from the enemy
and receive me at the hour of my death.

Remember, O Most Gracious Virgin Mary
(Memorare)

Remember, O most gracious Virgin Mary,
that never was it known
that anyone who fled to your protection,
implored your help or sought your interces-
    sion,
was left unaided.
Inspired with this confidence,
I fly to you, O Virgin of virgins, my Mother;
to you do I come,
before you I stand, sinful and sorrowful.
O Mother of the Word Incarnate,
despise not my petitions,
but in your mercy hear and answer me.

Hail, Holy Queen
(Salve Regina)

Hail, holy Queen, Mother of mercy,
hail, our life, our sweetness, and our hope.
To you do we cry,
poor banished children of Eve.
To you do we send up our sighs,
mourning and weeping in this valley of tears.

Turn then, most gracious Advocate,
your eyes of mercy toward us.
And after this our exile
show unto us the blessed fruit of your womb,
    Jesus.
O clement, O loving, O sweet Virgin Mary.

Prayer of Consecration to Mary

O my Queen and Mother,
I give myself entirely to you.
To show my devotion to you
I consecrate to you this day
my eyes, ears, mouth, heart,
and whole being without reserve.

Therefore, good Mother,
since I am your own,
keep me and guard me
as your property and possession.

The Angel of the Lord

(Angelus Domini)

a) *During the year* (outside of the Easter Season)

℣. The Angel of the Lord declared unto Mary,
℟. And she conceived of the Holy Spirit.

Hail Mary.

℣. Behold the handmaid of the Lord,
℟. Be it done unto me according to your word.

Hail Mary.

℣. And the Word was made flesh,
℟. And dwelt among us.

Hail Mary.

℣. Pray for us, O holy Mother of God,
℟. That we may be made worthy of the promises of Christ.

Let us pray. Pour forth, we beg You, O Lord,
Your grace into our hearts:
that we, to whom the Incarnation of Christ Your Son
was made known by the message of an Angel,
may by His Passion and Cross
be brought to the glory of His Resurrection.
Through the same Christ our Lord.

Queen of Heaven

(Regina Caeli)

b) *During the Easter Season*

Queen of Heaven, rejoice, alleluia:
For He Whom you merited to bear, alleluia,
Has risen, as He said, alleluia.
Pray for us to God, alleluia.

℣. Rejoice and be glad, O Virgin Mary, alleluia.

℟. Because the Lord is truly risen, alleluia.

Let us pray. O God, Who by the Resurrection of Your Son,
our Lord Jesus Christ,
granted joy to the whole world:
grant, we beg You,
that through the intercession of the Virgin Mary, His Mother,
we may lay hold of the joys of eternal life.
Through the same Christ our Lord.

Holy Mary, Help the Helpless

Holy Mary,
help the helpless,
strengthen the fearful,
comfort the sorrowful,
pray for the people,
plead for the clergy,
intercede for all women consecrated to God;
may all who keep your sacred commemoration
experience the might of your assistance.

Prayer of Praise—Inviolata

O Mary,
you are inviolate,
pure and without stain,
you who became the glistening gate of heaven.
O most dear and gracious Mother of Jesus,
receive our modest songs of praise.

We beg you with heart and lips:
make our bodies and souls pure.
By your sweet prayers,
obtain eternal pardon for us.
O Mother most kind! O Queen! O Mary!
who alone remained inviolate!

Prayer for the Grace to Love Jesus

Mary, my dear Mother,
how much I love you—
and yet in reality how little!
You teach me what I should know,
for you instruct me in
what Jesus is for me
and what I should be for Him.

O my beloved Mother,
how close to God you are,
and how completely filled with Him!
To the extent that we know God,
we are reminded of you.

Mother of God,
obtain for me the grace of loving my Jesus
and the grace of loving you.

Prayer to See Jesus through Mary

Most holy and immaculate Virgin,
my Mother!
You are the Mother of my Lord,
the Queen of the universe,
the advocate, hope, and refuge of sinners.

I, the most miserable of sinners,
have recourse to you today.
I venerate you, great Queen,
and I thank you for the many graces
you have bestowed on me until now.
I thank you especially for having saved me
    from hell
which I have so often deserved by my many
    sins.

Most lovable Lady,
I love you,
and by the love I have for you
I promise to serve you always
and to do all I can to make you loved by others.
I place in you all my hope of salvation.
Mother of mercy,
receive me as your servant
and cover me with the mantle of your protec-
    tion.
Since you are so powerful with God,
deliver me from all temptations
or rather obtain for me the grace
to overcome them until death.

I ask of you a true love for Jesus Christ.
Through you I hope to die a good death.
My dear Mother,
by the love you have for almighty God
I beg you to help me always
and especially at the last moment of my life.
Do not leave me until you see me safe in heaven,
where I hope to thank and praise you forever.

Prayer of Dedication to Mary

Virgin full of goodness,
Mother of mercy,
I entrust to you my body and my soul,
my thoughts and my actions,
my life and my death.

O my Queen,
come to my aid
and deliver me from the snares of the devil.
Obtain for me the grace of loving
my Lord Jesus Christ, your Son,
with a true and perfect love,
and after Him, O Mary,
of loving you with all my heart
and above all things.

Litany of Loreto

Lord, have mercy.
Christ, have mercy.
Lord, have mercy.
Christ, hear us.
Christ, *graciously hear us,*
God, the Father of heaven,
  have mercy on us.
God the Son, Redeemer of
  the world,
  have mercy on us.
God, the Holy Spirit,
  have mercy on us.
Holy Trinity, one God,
  have mercy on us.
Holy Mary, *pray for us.* *
Holy Mother of God,

Holy Virgin of virgins,
Mother of Christ,
Mother of the Church,
Mother of Divine grace,
Mother most pure,
Mother most chaste,
Mother inviolate,
Mother undefiled,
Mother most amiable,
Mother most admirable,
Mother of good counsel,
Mother of our Creator,
Mother of our Savior,
Virgin most prudent,
Virgin most venerable,
Virgin most renowned,

* *Pray for us* is repeated after each invocation.

Virgin most powerful,
Virgin most merciful,
Virgin most faithful,
Mirror of justice,
Seat of wisdom,
Cause of our joy,
Spiritual vessel,
Vessel of honor,
Singular vessel of devotion,
Mystical rose,
Tower of David,
Tower of ivory,
House of gold,
Ark of the covenant,
Gate of heaven,
Morning star,
Health of the sick,
Refuge of sinners,
Comforter of the afflicted,
Help of Christians,
Queen of angels,
Queen of patriarchs,
Queen of prophets,
Queen of apostles,
Queen of martyrs,
Queen of confessors,

Queen of virgins,
Queen of all saints,
Queen conceived without original sin,
Queen assumed into heaven,
Queen of the most holy Rosary,
Queen of families,
Queen of peace,

Lamb of God, You take away the sins of the world; *spare us, O Lord!*

Lamb of God, You take away the sins of the world; *graciously hear us, O Lord!*

Lamb of God, You take away the sins of the world; *have mercy on us.*

℣. Pray for us, O holy Mother of God.

℟. *That we may be made worthy of the promises of Christ.*

Let us pray.
Grant, we beg You, O Lord God,
that we Your servants
may enjoy lasting health of mind and body,
and by the glorious intercession
of the Blessed Mary, ever Virgin,
be delivered from present sorrow
and enter into the joy of eternal happiness.
Through Christ our Lord.
℟. *Amen.*

Contemporary Prayers

Biblical Litany of Our Lady

Greeted by the angel Gabriel: Lk 1:28.
Full of Grace: *ibid.*
Mother of Jesus: Lk 1:31.
Mother of the Son of the Most High: Lk 1:32.
Mother of the son of David: *ibid.*
Mother of the King of Israel: Lk 1:33.
Mother by act of the Holy Spirit: Lk 1:35; Mt 1:20.
Handmaid of the Lord: Lk 1:38.
Virgin, Mother of Emmanuel: Mt 1:23, citing Isa 7:14; see Mt 5:2.
You in whom the Word became flesh: Jn 1:14.
You in whom the Word dwelt among us: *ibid.*
Blessed among all women: Lk 1:41; see Jud 13:18.
Mother of the Lord: Lk 1:43.
Happy are you who have believed in the words uttered by the Lord: Lk 1:43.
Lowly handmaid of the Lord: Lk 1:48.
Called blessed by all generations: *ibid.*
You in whom the Almighty worked wonders: *ibid.*
Heiress of the promises made to Abraham: Lk 1:55.
Mother of the new Isaac: Lk 1:37 (Gen 18:14).
You who gave birth to your firstborn at Bethlehem: Lk 2:7.

You who wrapped your Child in swaddling clothes and laid Him in a manger: *ibid.*

Woman from whom Jesus was born: Gal 4:4; Mt 1:16, 21.

Mother of the Savior: Lk 2:11; Mt 1:21.

Mother of the Messiah: Lk 2:11; Mt 1:16.

You who were found by the shepherds with Joseph and the newborn Child: Lk 2:16.

You who kept and meditated all things in your heart: Lk 2:19.

You who offered Jesus in the Temple: Lk 2:22.

You who put Jesus into the arms of Simeon: Lk 2:28.

You who marvelled at what was said of Jesus: Lk 2:33.

You whose soul a sword should pierce: Lk 2:35.

Mother who were found together with the Child by the Wise Men: Mt 2:11.

Mother whom Joseph took into refuge in Egypt: Mt 2:14.

You who took the Child Jesus to Jerusalem for the Passover: Lk 2:42.

You who searched for Jesus for three days: Lk 2:46.

You who found Jesus again in His Father's house: Lk 2:46-49.

Mother whom Jesus obeyed at Nazareth: Lk 2:51.

Model of widows: see Mk 6:3.

Jesus' companion at the marriage feast at Cana: Jn 2:1-2.

You who told the servants, "Do as He shall tell you": Jn 2:5.

You who gave rise to Jesus' first miracle: Jn 2:11.

Mother of Jesus for having done the will of the Father in heaven: Mt 12:50.

Mary who chose the better part: Lk 10:42.

Blessed for having heard the word of God and kept it: Lk 11:28.

Mother standing at the foot of the Cross: Jn 19:25.

Mother of the disciple whom Jesus loved: Jn 19:26-27.

Queen of the Apostles, persevering in prayer with them: Acts 1:14.

Woman clothed with the sun: Rev 12:1.

Woman crowned with twelve stars: *ibid.*

Sorrowful Mother of the Church: Rev 12:2.

Glorious Mother of the Messiah: Rev 12:5.

Image of the new Jerusalem: Rev 21:2.

River of living water, flowing from the throne of God and the Lamb: Rev 22:1. See Ps 45:5.

Prayer to Mary, Mother of the Church

O Blessed Virgin Mary,
the basic reason why you are Mother of the Church
is that you are the Mother of God
and the associate of Christ in His saving work.
Another reason is that you shine as the model of virtues
for the whole community of the elect.

You exemplified in your own life
the beatitudes preached by your Divine Son.
Hence, you are the perfect model
for the imitation of Christ
on the part of all human beings.

Obtain for us the graces we need
to follow your example.
Teach us to practice the beatitudes proper to
    our state
and to rejoice in being known as your children
who are members of the Church of God.
Let us work for the unity of the Church,
which your Son desired on earth
and which you now pray for in heaven.
Lead the whole human race
to acknowledge Christ Jesus, the one true
    Savior.
Drive from it all the calamities provoked by
    sin,
and bring it that peace which consists
in truth, justice, liberty, and love.

Prayer to Emulate Mary's Faith

Mary our Mother,
you consented in faith
to become the Mother of Jesus.
At the Angel's announcement
you received the Word of God in your heart
as well as in your body,
and you brought Life to the world.

You conceived in your heart, with your whole
being,
before you conceived in your womb.

Obtain for us
a faith similar to your own,
which will enable us to hear the Word of God
and carry it out.
Let us imitate your Motherhood by our faith,
bringing Christ to birth in others
who have desperate need of Him.

Prayer to Mary Assumed into Heaven

O Blessed Virgin Mary,
united to the victorious Christ in heaven,
you are the image and first-flowering of the
Church
as she is to be perfected in the world to come.
You shine forth as a sign of sure hope and
solace
for the pilgrim People of God.

In your Assumption,
you manifest the fullness of Redemption
and appear as the spotless image of the
Church
responding in joy to the invitation of the
Bridegroom,
your Son,
Who is the firstfruits of those who have fall-
en asleep.

Grant that we may follow your example on
   earth
thereby imitating your Son as well
and being enabled to share your glory
with Him for all eternity.

Prayer to Mary, Queen of the Home

O Blessed Virgin Mary,
you are the Mother and Queen of every Christian family.
When you conceived and gave birth to Jesus,
human motherhood reached its greatest
   achievement.
From the time of the Annunciation
you were the living chalice
of the Son of God made Man.
You are the Queen of the home.
As a woman of faith,
you inspire all mothers to transmit faith
to their children.

Watch over our families.
Let the children learn free and loving obedience
inspired by your obedience to God.
Let parents learn dedication and selflessness
based on your unselfish attitude.
Let all families honor you
and remain devoted to you
so that they may be held together
by your example and your intercession.

The Litany of the Blessed Virgin Mary

The following litany is part of the newly approved Order of Crowning an Image of the Blessed Virgin Mary. *The core of the litany lies in its explanation of Mary's Queenship.*

Lord, have mercy.
Lord, have mercy.
Christ, have mercy.
Christ, have mercy.
Lord, have mercy.
Lord, have mercy.

God, our Father in heaven, *have mercy on us.*
God the Son, Redeemer of the world, *have mercy on us.*
God, the Holy Spirit, *have mercy on us.*
Holy Trinity, one God, *have mercy on us.*

Holy Mary, *pray for us.* *
Holy Mother of God,
Most honored of virgins,

Chosen daughter of the Father,
Mother of Christ the King,
Glory of the Holy Spirit,

Virgin daughter of Zion,
Virgin poor and humble,
Virgin gentle and obedient,

Handmaid of the Lord,
Mother of the Lord,
Helper of the Redeemer,

Full of grace,
Fountain of beauty,
Model of virtue,

Finest fruit of the redemption,
Perfect disciple of Christ,
Untarnished image of the Church,

Woman transformed,
Woman clothed with the sun,
Woman crowned with stars,

Gentle Lady,
Gracious Lady,
Our Lady,

Joy of Israel,
Splendor of the Church,
Pride of the human race,

Advocate of grace,
Minister of holiness,
Champion of God's people,

Queen of love,
Queen of mercy,
Queen of peace,

Queen of angels,
Queen of patriarchs and prophets,
Queen of apostles and martyrs,
Queen of confessors and virgins,

Queen of all saints,
Queen conceived without sin,

* *Pray for us* is repeated after each invocation.

Queen assumed into heaven,

Queen of all the earth,
Queen of heaven,
Queen of the universe,

Lamb of God, You take away the sins of the world; *spare us, O Lord.*
Lamb of God, You take away the sins of the world; *hear us, O Lord.*

Lamb of God, You take away the sins of the world; *have mercy on us.*

℣. Pray for us, O glorious Mother of the Lord.

℟. *That we may become worthy of the promises of Christ.*

Let us pray.
God of mercy,
listen to the prayers of Your servants
who have honored Your handmaid Mary as
  Mother and Queen.
Grant that by Your grace
we may serve You and our neighbor on earth
and be welcomed into Your eternal kingdom.
We ask this through Christ our Lord.
℟. *Amen.*

Prayer in Union with the Seven Words of Mary

Mary, Mother of Wisdom,
in the Gospels
we have only seven of your words,
but they are filled with wisdom
and are spirit and life.
I wish to reflect on them
in accord with the Divine admonition:
"Keep your mother's words fastened
over your heart always" (Prov 6:21).

First Word: Childlike Wonder

Mary, when the Angel Gabriel announced to
    you
that you were to be the Mother of God,
you responded with a word of *childlike wonder:*
"How can this be
since I do not know man?" (Lk 1:34).
This *first word* tells me to look at life
with my eyes of faith wide open.
At every moment and in every circumstance
God is really calling out to me.

Dearest Mother,
help me to keep myself open to God's call
and to see Him in the framework of my every-
    day life.
For in each circumstance I have something to
    give
that is exclusively my own.

Second Word: Obedient Service

Mary,
when the Angel assured you
that your virginity would remain intact
since you would conceive by the power of
    God,
you responded with a word of *obedient service:*
"I am the servant of the Lord" (Lk 1:38).
This *second word* encourages me
to be really obedient to God's call.
The best way to do so is
in union with the Church.

Dearest Mother,
help me to be in tune with the Church,
to love the Church,
and to cherish the Church as God's gift.

Third Word: Biblical Knowledge

Mary,
on that same occasion you went further
and added a word of *Biblical knowledge:*
"Let it be done to me according to your word"
    (Lk 1:38).
This *third word* urges me
to seek Biblical knowledge and understanding.

Dearest Mother,
help me to love the Bible
and read it diligently.
Let me regard it
as the unique revelation of God
and be willing to learn
the characteristics of the Bible,
the attitude inculcated by the Bible,
and the mentality endorsed by the Bible.

Fourth Word: Joyful Praise

Mary,
upon your visitation to Elizabeth,
you uttered a word of *joyful praise:*
"My soul proclaims the greatness of the Lord . . ."
    (Lk 1:46-55).
This *fourth word* reminds me
that I am to offer spiritual worship

for the glory of God
and the salvation of human beings.

Dearest Mother,
help me to tune into the Spirit
Who prepares us to offer worship to God
in spirit and in truth.
Enable me to offer
all my works, prayers, and apostolic endeavors
as well as my family life and daily occupation,
my physical and mental relaxation,
and even my hardships in life.
Let me offer them in the Eucharist
together with your Divine Son Himself,
and so consecrate the world to God.

Fifth Word: Gentle Authority

Mary,
on finding Jesus in the Temple,
you uttered a word of *gentle authority:*
"Son, why have You done this to us?
You see that Your father and I have been look-
   ing for You
in sorrow" (Lk 2:48).
This *fifth word* brings out your gentleness
and your acceptance of the responsibility and
   authority
that God has given you.
It is a vivid reminder
that we have a role to play
in bringing about the Kingdom of God
that Jesus proclaimed by word and deed.

Dearest Mother,
help me to announce Christ to others
by presenting a living testimony to Him,
by cultivating a solid and genuine faith
in His teachings given by the Church,
and by cooperating fully in the special grace
He has given me to carry out what is useful
for the building up of the Church.

Sixth Word: Tender Charity

Mary,
at the wedding feast of Cana,
you uttered a word of *tender charity:*
"They have no more wine" (Jn 2:3).
This *sixth word* demonstrates the greatness
of your Heart.
It reminds me that I am called
to serve Christ in my fellow human beings,
so that I may
by humility and patience
lead them to the Kingdom of God.

Dearest Mother,
help me to learn the meaning and value
of all creation
as well as its role in the harmonious praise of
     God.
To do so,
enable me to assist others
to live holier lives each day,
so that the world will be permeated
by the Spirit of Christ

and may effectively fulfill its purposes
in justice, charity, and peace.

Seventh Word: Operative Faith

Mary,
after informing Jesus
of the bridal couple's problem at Cana
you uttered a word of *operative faith:*
"Do whatever [Jesus] tells you" (Jn 2:5).
This *seventh word* exhibits the faith
that has made you the first among believers.
As Abraham is the father of our faith,
you are the Mother of our faith.

Dearest Mother,
help me to have an operative faith,
a faith that does not lie dormant
but leads to works.
Enable me to believe
that God is personally concerned with me,
that He communicates with me,
that He sent His Son to save me,
and that He has a plan in everything that hap-
   pens to me.

O Mother of Wisdom,
inscribe your words on my heart
and keep them ever in my mind.
Let them remind me of you
and inspire me to call upon you.
Grant that they may lead me
to the throne of your Divine Son
where I hope to obtain eternal pardon and peace
because of your interceding word with Jesus.

MARY AND THE PRAYERS OF THE CHURCH—
Mary was present with the disciples in prayer at the
birth of the Church. The Church has always prayed
with her, in her honor, and to her in the Liturgy, the
public prayer of the Body of Christ.

PRAYERS FROM THE LITURGY

The Liturgy is one of the best sources of prayers to our Lady. The Church makes place for Mary in the public prayer of the Body of Christ. And she does so in three different but related ways of praying.

The Church prays to God with Mary. *She takes cognizance of Mary hearing and receiving the Word of God or repeats Mary's canticle of thanksgiving. She also identifies herself with Mary in the offering of Christ's sacrifice on the Cross or has recourse (at least indirectly) to Mary's intercession in heaven.*

The Church prays to God in honor of Mary. *She "celebrates" the Virgin Mary by praising the Lord for the participation of the Mother of Jesus in the major events of her Son's life. The Church also gives praise to God for the special graces that prepared the Virgin Mary for her mission and for the rewards heaped upon her in body and soul as well as for a number of events in the life of God's people where Mary's action was particularly evident. Each time also provides the Church with an occasion for recourse to Mary's intercession so that the faithful might follow her example or enjoy her protection.*

The Church prays to Mary. She speaks directly not to God but to Mary herself, to praise her, to congratulate her in words of the Gospel, but also in direct recourse to her intercession.

In none of these forms is the prayer to Mary considered an end in itself. Yet it remains eminently suitable to serve the worship owed to the true God alone. The Father receives honor and praise for the wisdom of His purposes revealed to Mary. Through the honor paid to His Mother, the Son is better known and loved. And the action of the Spirit in Mary and the Church also is extolled and proclaimed.

Above all, we must remember that Mary's mediation is not additional to that of Christ, since Mary and Christ are but one in the Mystery of His Mystical Body. But to those who pray to her, she brings the Motherly help of her own prayer, which merges with the supreme prayer of Christ the Mediator.

Western Church

Living Memory of Mary

In communion with those whose memory we venerate,
especially the glorious ever-Virgin Mary,
Mother of our God and Lord, Jesus Christ,
and blessed Joseph, her Spouse,

your blessed Apostles and Martyrs,
Peter and Paul, Andrew,
(James, John,
Thomas, James, Philip,
Bartholomew, Matthew,
Simon and Jude;
Linus, Cletus, Clement, Sixtus,
Cornelius, Cyprian,
Lawrence, Chrysogonus,
John and Paul,
Cosmas and Damian)
and all your Saints;
we ask that through their merits and prayers,
in all things we may be defended
by your protecting help.
(Through Christ our Lord. Amen.)

Communicantes of Roman Canon

Prayer for Forgiveness

I confess to almighty God
and to you, my brothers and sisters,
that I have greatly sinned,
in my thoughts and in my words,
in what I have done and in what I have
    failed to do,
through my fault, through my fault,
through my most grievous fault;
therefore I ask blessed Mary ever-Virgin,
all the Angels and Saints,
and you, my brothers and sisters,
to pray for me to the Lord our God.

Penitential Act at Mass

Mary, Associate of Christ in the Redemption

It is truly right and just, our duty and our salvation,
always and everywhere to give you thanks,
Lord, holy Father, almighty and eternal God,
through Christ our Lord.
For in your loving providence
you decreed that Mary, the Mother of your
Son,
should stand faithfully beside his Cross,
and so fulfill in her person
the prophecies of old,
and enrich the world
with her own witness of living faith.
At the Cross the Blessed Virgin appears as the
new Eve,
so that, as a woman shared in bringing death,
so a woman would share in restoring life.
At the Cross with motherly love
she embraces her scattered children,
reunited through the Death of Christ,
and she fulfills the mystery of the mother of
Zion.
At the Cross she stands
as the model of the Church, the Bride of
Christ,
which draws inspiration from her courage
and keeps constant faith with its Bridegroom,
undaunted by peril and unbroken by persecution.

In our joy we sing to your glory
with all the choirs of Angels.

Preface for Mass of Mary at the Foot of the Cross I

Mary, Seat of Wisdom

O happy Virgin,
you gave birth to the Lord;
O blessed seat of Wisdom,
you cradle in our hearts
the Spirit of your Son Jesus Christ.

Gospel Acclamation for Mass of Mary Seat of Wisdom

Mary, Cause of Our Joy

Hail, holy Mary,
joy of humankind,
remaining a virgin, you gave birth
and brought forth for us
the One who is our salvation and joy.

Gospel Acclamation for Mass of Mary, Cause of Our Joy

The Magnificat

My soul proclaims the greatness of the Lord,
my spirit rejoices in God my Savior
for He has looked with favor on His lowly
servant.

From this day all generations will call me
blessed.
The Almighty has done great things for me,
and holy is His Name.

He has mercy on those who fear Him
in every generation.

He has shown the strength of His arm,
He has scattered the proud in their conceit.

He has cast down the mighty from their
   thrones,
and has lifted up the lowly.

He has filled the hungry with good things,
and the rich He has sent away empty.

He has come to the help of His servant Israel
for He has remembered His promise of mercy,
the promise He made to our fathers,
to Abraham and his children for ever.

Divine Office: Evening Prayer

At the Cross Her Station Keeping
(Stabat Mater)

At the Cross her station keeping,
Stood the mournful Mother weeping,
Close to Jesus to the last.
Through her heart, His sorrow sharing,
All His bitter anguish bearing,
Lo, the piercing sword has passed!

O, how sad and sore distressed,
Was that Mother highly blessed
Of the sole-begotten One.
Christ above in torment hangs,
She beneath beholds the pangs
Of her dying glorious Son.

Is there one who would not weep
'Whelmed in miseries so deep
Christ's dear Mother to behold?
Can the human heart refrain

From partaking in the pain
In that Mother's pain untold?

Bruised, derided, cursed, defiled,
She beheld her tender Child,
All with bloody scourges rent.
For the sins of His own nation
Saw Him hang in desolation
Till His Spirit forth He sent.

O sweet Mother! fount of love,
Touch my spirit from above,
Make my heart with yours accord.
Make me feel as you have felt.
Make my soul to glow and melt
With the love of Christ, my Lord.

Holy Mother, pierce me through.
In my heart each wound renew
Of my Savior crucified.
Let me share with you His pain,
Who for all our sins was slain,
Who for me in torments died.

Let me mingle tears with you
Mourning Him Who mourned for me,
All the days that I may live.
By the Cross with you to stay,
There with you to weep and pray,
Is all I ask of you to give.

Virgin of all virgins blest!
Listen to my fond request:
Let me share your grief divine.
Let me, to my latest breath,

In my body bear the Death
Of your dying Son divine.

Wounded with His every wound,
Steep my soul till it has swooned
In His very Blood away.
Be to me, O Virgin, nigh,
Lest in flames I burn and die,
In His awe-full judgment day.

Christ, when You shall call me hence,
Be Your Mother my defense,
Be Your Cross my victory.
While my body here decays,
May my soul Your goodness praise,
Safe in heaven eternally.
Amen. Alleluia.

Sequence for Mass of Our Lady of Sorrows

Mary the Dawn

Mary the Dawn, Christ the Perfect Day;
Mary the Gate, Christ the Heavenly Way!

Mary the Root, Christ the Mystic Vine;
Mary the Grape, Christ the Sacred Wine!

Mary the Wheat, Christ the Living-Bread;
Mary the Stem, Christ the Rose blood-red!

Mary the Font, Christ the Cleansing Flood;
Mary the Cup, Christ the Saving Blood!

Mary the Temple, Christ the Temple's Lord;
Mary the Shrine, Christ the God adored!

Mary the Beacon, Christ the Haven's Rest;
Mary the Mirror, Christ the Vision Blest!

Mary the Mother, Christ the Mother's Son
By all things blest while endless ages run.
  Amen.   Divine Office

Mother Benign of Our Redeeming Lord
(Alma Redemptoris Mater)

Mother benign of our redeeming Lord,
Star of the sea and portal of the skies,
Unto your fallen people help afford—
Fallen, but striving still anew to rise.

You who did once, while wondering worlds
  adored,
Bear your Creator, Virgin then as now,
O by your holy joy at Gabriel's word,
Pity the sinners who before you bow.
                                          Divine Office

Hail, Holy Queen
See p. 12.

Hail, O Queen of Heaven
(Ave Regina Caelorum)

Hail, O Queen of heaven enthroned!
Hail, by angels Mistress owned!
Root of Jesse, Gate of morn,
Whence the world's true Light was born.

Glorious Virgin, joy to you,
Loveliest whom in heaven they view:
Fairest where all are fair,
Plead with Christ our sins to spare. Divine Office

O Mary, of All Women

O Mary, of all women
You are the chosen one,
Who, ancient Prophets promised,
Would bear God's only Son;
All Hebrew generations
Prepared the way to thee,
That in your womb the God-Man
Might come to set man free.

O Mary, you embody
All God taught to our race,
For you are first and foremost
In fullness of His grace;
We praise this wondrous honor
That you gave birth to Him
Who from you took His manhood
And saved us from our sin.   Divine Office

O Most Holy One
(O Sanctissima)

O most holy one,
O most lowly one,
Dearest Virgin, Maria!
Mother of fair Love,
Home of the Spirit Dove,
Ora, ora pro nobis.

Help in sadness drear,
Port of gladness near,
Virgin Mother, Maria!
In pity heeding,

Hear thou our pleading,
Ora, ora pro nobis.

Mother, Maiden fair,
Look with loving care,
Hear our prayer, O Maria!
Our sorrow feeling,
Send us thy healing,
Ora, ora pro nobis!

Divine Office

The God Whom Earth and Sea and Sky

The God Whom earth and sea and sky
Adore and laud and magnify,
Whose might they own, whose praise they tell,
In Mary's body deigned to dwell.

O Mother blest! the chosen shrine,
Wherein the Architect Divine,
Whose hand contains the earth and sky,
Vouchsafed in hidden guise to lie.

Blest in the message Gabriel brought;
Blest by the work the Spirit wrought;
Most blest, to bring to human birth
The long-desired of all the earth.

O Lord, the Virgin-born, to Thee
Eternal praise and glory be,
Whom with the Father we adore
And Holy Spirit for evermore.

Divine Office

Eastern Church

Anaphora in Honor of Mary

Mary,
you are the extension of heaven
and the foundation of the earth,
the depths of the seas
and the light of the sun,
the beauty of the moon
and the splendor of the stars in the sky.
You are greater than the cherubim,
more eminent than the seraphim,
and more glorious than the chariot of fire.
Your womb bore God,
whose majesty overwhelms human beings.
Your lap held the glowing coal.
Your knees propped up the lion of august
   majesty.
Your hands touched the untouchable
and the fire of the Divinity that lies therein.
Your fingers are like the incandescent tongs
with which the Prophet received the coal of the
   heavenly oblation.
You are the basket of this bread of burning
   flame
and the chalice of this wine.

O Mary,
you produce in your womb the fruit of the
   offering.
We your servants of this sanctuary
ask you to guard us

from the enemy that attacks us,
so that as the water and wine are not sepa-
    rated in their mixture,
we too will not be separated from you
and your Son, the Lamb of salvation.

Ethiopic Anaphora

Mother of Life

In your Motherhood you preserved your vir-
    ginity,
and in your dormition you did not abandon
    the world,
O Mother of God.

You passed on to life,
since you are the Mother of Life.
By your intercession,
free our souls from death.

Byzantine Office for the Assumption

Hail, Full of Grace

In your Motherhood, the conception was not
    caused by man,
and in your dormition, death did not lead to
    corruption.
Mother of God,
you have gone from one prodigy to another.

Indeed, how could one who did not know
    matrimony
nourish a child in her womb and remain a
    virgin?

And how can the Mother of God be anointed
  with spices
as if she were dead?
Hence, we exclaim with the Angel
"Hail, full of grace."

Byzantine Office for the Assumption

Prayer for Help against Evil

Oppressed by sin and sadness,
we have recourse to the Mother of God.
Filled with sorrow for our sins,
we kneel and cry from the depths of our hearts:
O our Queen, come to our aid.
Have compassion on us.
We are overwhelmed to the point of succumb-
  ing
under the weight of our sins.
Do not disillusion your servants,
for you are our only hope.

Mother of God,
even though we are unworthy to receive your
  aid,
we will never cease making your power known.
If you should not be here to intercede for us,
who would free us from such dangers?
Who could have preserved us unharmed until
  now?
Our Queen,
we will never go far from you,
for you always save your servants
from all their misfortunes.

Prayer in Time of Trial

All holy Lady,
do not abandon me to the power of human
  beings.
Hear the plea of your servant
for I am oppressed by anguish
and find it difficult to resist the pressures of
  evil.
I have no defense
and I do not know where to flee.
I am assailed on all sides
and I find no consolation except in you.
Queen of the world,
hope and protection of the faithful,
do not despise my petition
but grant me what I need.

Byzantine Liturgy

Mother of the Lamb

Hail (*or* Rejoice), Mother of the Lamb and the
  Shepherd.
Hail (*or* Rejoice), sheepfold of the spiritual
  flocks.
Hail (*or* Rejoice), shelter against invisible
  enemies.
Hail (*or* Rejoice), entrance to the gates of
  paradise.
Hail (*or* Rejoice), because heaven embraces
  earth.
Hail (*or* Rejoice), because earth sings together
  with heaven.

Hail (*or* Rejoice), perennial voice of the Apostles.

Hail (*or* Rejoice), unshakable courage of the Martyrs.

Hail (*or* Rejoice), solid bulwark of the faith.

Hail (*or* Rejoice), radiant sign of grace.

Hail (*or* Rejoice), you through whom hell was rendered armorless.

Hail (*or* Rejoice), you through whom we were reinvested with glory.

Hail (*or* Rejoice), O immaculate Bride.

Akathist Hymn

Mother of Life

How can we fail, O all-holy one,
to admire your Divine and human childbearing!
O all immaculate one,
without the help of a man,
you brought into the world
a Son Who has no father according to the flesh.

He is the Word begotten in eternity by the Father,
without mother.
He suffered no change, admixture, or division
but integrally retained the characteristics of each nature.

O Lady and Virgin Mother,
beseech Him to save the souls of those who,
in true faith,
acknowledge you as the Mother of God.

The Prophet David,
who, for your sake, was an ancestor of the
   God-Man,
addressed the following words, in his hymns,
to the One Who has done great things in you:
"The Queen takes her place
at Your right hand" (Ps 45:10).

God has chosen you to be
the productive Mother of life.
He became a human being in you,
without a human father,
in order to restore in human beings
the image of Himself that had been tarnished
   by sin.
He did so to lead back to His Father
the little sheep lost on the mountains,
carrying it on His shoulders,
to reunite humankind with the Powers of
   heaven,
and so save the world,
O Mother of Christ the Lord
Who is rich in mercy!   *Byzantine Liturgy*

Star Illumined by the Sun

Hail, Star illumined by the sun, hail:
through you creation has been renewed.

You are the heavenly Stairway
through which God has descended.

You are the Earth
of the fruit that never perishes.

You are the Key
to the doors of paradise.

You are the burning Bush
that is not consumed.

You are the Sea
that drowns the spiritual Pharaoh.

You are the Rock
that gives forth water for the thirsty.

You are the Column of Fire
that guides those who are in darkness.

You are the Nutriment
that has replaced the manna.

You are the Promised Land
flowing with milk and honey.

You are the Tabernacle of God
and the Word.

You are the Ark
gilded by the Holy Spirit.

You are the Censer of gold and perfume
giving forth the holy fragrance of Christ.

Byzantine Liturgy

All-Holy Servant and Mother

O All-holy Servant and Mother
of the Divine Word,
childbirth revealed you to be a virgin
and virginity made you fruitful.

Gather in your devout embrace
the people who have recourse to you.

In your profound mercy
take care of the flock
that was redeemed by the Blood of the Son
Whom you have brought forth.

Show yourself a Mother to creatures,
for you gave nourishment to their Creator.
Bless with your service those whom you see
offering themselves to you in homage.

Grant that we may be protected by your
intercession
for we exult in bearing
the sweet yoke of your servitude.

And grant that all of us who have sung praises
in honor of your conception
may continue to live in your service,
so that once the stain of sin has been removed
we may attain the One
Whose Mother we honor you to be
by our celebrations.

Defend us now and forever
with your inexhaustible affection
so that the One Whom you brought forth
may possess us eternally in His Kingdom.

Visigothic Book of Prayer

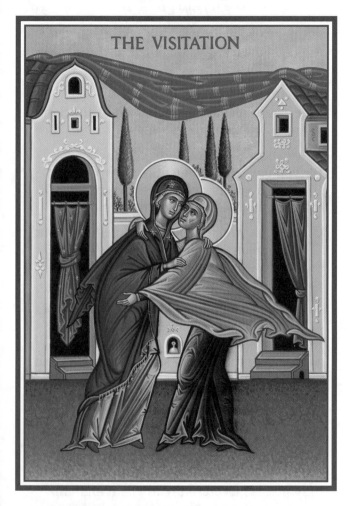

THE VISITATION

THE SAINTS AND MARY—The Saints have always been in the vanguard of those devoted to Mary. They faithfully mirror the Tradition of the Church in their prayers to Mary.

PRAYERS FROM
CHURCH TRADITION

This section contains prayers taken from the Tradition of the Church apart from the Liturgy. More particularly, it contains the prayers of those who best represent that Tradition—the Saints (including some Popes).

The Saints are images of God. They have put on Christ completely. To use the words of the early Christians of Smyrna: "We adore Christ because He is the Son of God; we love the Saints because they are disciples and imitators of our Lord."

This has been the unchanging position of the Church toward the Saints, who embrace all states of life: ascetics, clergy, missionaries, laity. Each of them bears the image of God and reveals some trait of Jesus.

In a St. Augustine of Hippo, we see Christ's art of instructing the people; in a St. Francis of Assisi, His overwhelming love for all creatures; in a St. Thomas Aquinas, His unparalleled wisdom. In a St. Gertrude of Helfta, we glimpse our Lord's life of inner prayer; in a St. Catherine of Siena, His common sense; in a St. Theresa of the Child Jesus, His acceptance of suffering for others.

In all of the Saints, we perceive Christ's overwhelming love and devotion to His Holy Mother.

The Saints are our models and intercessors. In the Preface for Holy Men and Women the Church prays: "In their lives on earth You give us their friendship. In their prayer for the Church You give strength and protection." Hence they are our models by their prayers as well as their actions.

Most of the prayers of the Saints to Mary found in this section have become classics and can be used by us with much fruit. They are filled with true Catholic teaching about Mary, loving reverence for the Mother of God, understanding of human nature, and beauty of language. They are a sure means to increase our devotion to our Lady and get closer to her Divine Son.

Prayers of Saints

Mary, Vessel of God's Mysteries

Mary,
you are the vessel and tabernacle containing
  all Mysteries.
You know what the Patriarchs never knew.
You have experienced what was never
  revealed to the Angels.

You have heard what the Prophets never heard.

In a word, all that was hidden from the preceding generations

was made known to you.

Even more, most of these wonders depended on you.   St. Gregory the Wonderworker (d. 270)

Mary, Mother of Grace

It becomes you to be mindful of us,

as you stand near Him Who granted you all graces,

for you are the Mother of God

and our Queen.

Help us for the sake of the King,

the Lord God and Master Who was born of you.

For this reason you are called full of grace.

Remember us,

most holy Virgin,

and bestow on us gifts from the riches of your graces,

Virgin full of grace.   St. Athanasius (d. 373)

Mary, Our Hope

Blessed Virgin, immaculate and pure,

you are the sinless Mother of your Son,

the mighty Lord of the universe.

You are holy and inviolate,

the hope of the hopeless and the sinful;

we sing your praises.

We praise you as full of every grace,
for you bore the God-Man.
We all venerate you;
we invoke you and implore your aid.

Holy and immaculate Virgin,
rescue us from every need that presses upon us
and from all the temptations of the devil.
Be our intercessor and advocate
at the hour of death and judgment.
Deliver us from the fire that is not extinguished
and from the outer darkness.

Make us worthy of the glory of your Son,
O dearest and most kind Virgin Mother.
You indeed are our most secure and only hope
for you are holy in the sight of God,
to Whom be honor and glory, majesty and
power forever.   St. Ephrem the Syrian (d. 373)

Mary, Mother of Mercy

Blessed Virgin Mary,
who can worthily repay you with praise and
thanks
for having rescued a fallen world
by your generous consent!
Receive our gratitude,
and by your prayers obtain the pardon of our
sins.
Take our prayers into the sanctuary of heaven
and enable them to make our peace with
God.

Holy Mary,
help the miserable,
strengthen the discouraged,
comfort the sorrowful,
pray for your people,
plead for the clergy,
intercede for all women consecrated to God.
May all who venerate you
feel now your help and protection.

Be ready to help us when we pray,
and bring back to us the answers to our
prayers.
Make it your continual concern
to pray for the people of God,
for you were blessed by God
and were made worthy
to bear the Redeemer of the world,
Who lives and reigns forever.

St. Augustine of Hippo (d. 430)

In Honor of Mary, Mother of God

Hail, Mary, Mother of God,
venerable treasure of the whole universe,
lamp that is never extinguished,
crown of virginity,
support of the true faith,
indestructible temple,
dwelling of Him Whom no place can contain,
O Mother and Virgin!

Through you
all the holy Gospels call blessed
the One Who comes in the name of the Lord.

Hail, Mother of God;
you enclosed under your Heart the infinite
 God
Whom no space can contain.
Through you
the Most Holy Trinity is adored and glorified,
and the priceless Cross is venerated
throughout the universe.

Through you
the heavens rejoice,
and the Angels and Archangels are filled with
 gladness.
Through you
the demons are banished,
and the tempter fell from heaven.
Through you
the fallen human race is admitted to heaven.

Hail, Mother of God;
through you
kings rule,
and the only-begotten Son of God
has become a star of light
to those who were sitting in darkness
and in the shadow of death.

St. Cyril of Alexandria (d. 444)

Mary, Model of Our Spiritual Life

Holy Virgin, I beg you:
enable me to receive Jesus from the Spirit,
according to the same process
by which you bore Jesus.

May my soul possess Jesus
thanks to the Spirit
through Whom you conceived Jesus.

May the grace to know Jesus
be granted to me through the Spirit
Who enabled you to know how to possess Jesus
and bring Him forth.

May my littleness show forth
the greatness of Jesus
in virtue of the Spirit
in Whom you recognized yourself
as the handmaid of the Lord,
desiring that it be done to you
according to the word of the Angel.

May I love Jesus
in the Spirit
in Whom you adored Him as your Lord
and looked after Him as your Son.

St. Ildefonsus of Toledo (d. 667)

Mary's Riches for Us

We are poor in Divine gifts,
O Mary,
but through you

we see the riches of kindness offered to us.
Therefore, we say with confidence:
the earth is full of the mercies of the Lord.

Rejected by God
because of the multitude of our sins,
through you we seek Him out again,
rediscover Him,
and are saved.

Therefore, O Mother of God,
grant us your powerful help
so that we may attain salvation.
And obtain for us the aid of your Son,
the sole Mediator necessary with God.

For your magnificence is infinite,
your goodness in helping the needy is inex-
    haustible,
and the number of your benefits is limitless.

No one achieves salvation except through
    you,
O most Immaculate One!
No one receives salvation except through you,
O most Chaste One!
And no one obtains mercy except through you,
O most Honored One!

Who would then fail to call you blessed?

I will call you—
who were enriched by your Son and God—
glorious and blessed,
and I will praise you with all generations.

St. Germanus of Constantinople (d. 732)

Mary, Hope of Christians

Hail Mary,
hope of Christians,
hear the prayer of a sinner who loves you
tenderly,
honors you in a special manner,
and places in you the hope of his/her salvation.
I owe you my life,
for you obtain for me the grace of your Son
and you are the sure pledge of my eternal
happiness.

I entreat you,
deliver me from the burden of my sins,
take away the darkness of my mind,
destroy the earthly affections of my heart,
defeat the temptations of my enemies,
and rule all the actions of my life.
With you as my guide
may I arrive at the eternal happiness of
heaven.   St. John Damascene (d. 754)

The Mother of God Is Our Mother

O Blessed Lady,
you are the Mother of Justification
and those who are justified;
the Mother of Reconciliation
and those who are reconciled;
the Mother of Salvation
and those who are saved.

What a blessed trust, and what a secure
refuge!

The Mother of God is our Mother.
The Mother of the One in Whom alone we
   hope
and Whom alone we fear
is our Mother! . . .

The One Who partook of our nature
and by restoring us to life
made us children of His Mother
invites us by this to proclaim
that we are His brothers and sisters.

Therefore, our Judge is also our Brother.
The Savior of the world is our Brother.
Our God has become—through Mary—our
   Brother!   St. Anselm of Canterbury (d. 1086)

Our Lady of the Trinity

Holy Virgin Mary,
there is none like you among women
born in the world.
Daughter and handmaid of the heavenly
   Father,
the almighty King,
Mother of our most high Lord Jesus Christ,
and Spouse of the Holy Spirit,
pray for us to your most holy Son,
our Lord and Master.

Hail, holy Lady,
most noble Queen,
Mother of God, and Mary ever Virgin.
You were chosen by the heavenly Father,

Who has been pleased to honor you
with the presence of His most holy Son
and the Divine Paraclete.

You were blessed with the fullness
of grace and goodness.
Hail, Temple of God,
His dwelling-place, His masterpiece, His
　hand-maid.
Hail, Mother of God.
I venerate you for the holy virtues that—
through the grace and light of the Holy
　Spirit—
you bring into the hearts of your clients
to change them from unfaithful Christians
to faithful children of God.

St. Francis of Assisi (d. 1126)

Mary Our Advocate

O blessed Lady, you found grace,
brought forth the Life,
and became the Mother of salvation.
May you obtain the grace for us to go to the
　Son.
By your mediation,
may we be received by the One
Who through you gave Himself to us.

May your integrity compensate with Him
for the fault of our corruption;
and may your humility, which is pleasing to
　God,
implore pardon for our vanity.

May your great charity cover the multitude
of our sins;
and may your glorious fecundity confer on us
a fecundity of merits.

Dear Lady,
our Mediatrix and Advocate,
reconcile us to your Son,
recommend us to Him,
and present us to your Son.

By the grace you found,
by the privilege you merited,
by the Mercy you brought forth,
obtain for us the following favor,
O blessed Lady.

May the One Who—thanks to you—came down
to share our infirmity and wretchedness
make us share—
again thanks to you—
His glory and beatitude:
Jesus Christ, your Son, our Lord,
Who reigns in heaven and is blessed forever!

St. Bernard of Clairvaux (d. 1153)

Mary Our Queen

Mary Our Queen,
Holy Mother of God,
we beg you to hear our prayer.
Make our hearts be filled with Divine grace
and resplendent with heavenly wisdom.
Render them strong with your might
and rich in virtue.

Pour down upon us the gift of mercy
so that we may obtain the pardon of our sins.
Help us to live in such a way
as to merit the glory and bliss of heaven.

May this be granted us by your Son Jesus
Who has exalted you above the Angels,
has crowned you as Queen,
and has seated you with Him forever on His
refulgent throne.   St. Anthony of Padua (d. 1231)

Prayer of Dedication to Mary

Virgin full of goodness,
Mother of mercy,
I entrust to you my body and my soul,
my thoughts and my actions,
my life and my death.
My Queen,
come to my aid
and deliver me from the snares of the devil.
Obtain for me the grace of loving
my Lord Jesus Christ, your Son,
with a true and perfect love,
and after Him,
O Mary,
of loving you with all my heart
and above all things.   St. Thomas Aquinas (d. 1274)

For a Happy Death

Holy Virgin,
I beg of you,

when my soul shall depart from my body,
be pleased to meet and receive it.

Mary,
do not refuse me then the grace
of being sustained by your sweet presence.
Be for me the ladder and the way to heaven,
and finally assure me of pardon and eternal
    rest.   St. Bonaventure (d. 1274)

Mother of Grace

"Do not be afraid, Mary,
for you have found favor with God" (Lk 1:30).
Fear not, Mary,
for you have found grace,
not taken it as Lucifer tried to do.
You have found grace,
not lost it as Adam did.
You have found favor with God
because you desired and sought it.
You have found uncreated Grace,
that is, God Himself became your Son,
and with that Grace
you have found and obtained every uncreated
    good.   St. Albert the Great (d. 1280)

Petition to Mary

Most chaste Virgin Mary,
by that spotless purity
with which you prepared for the Son of God
a dwelling of delight in your virginal womb,
I beg of you to intercede for me
that I may be cleansed from every stain.

Most humble Virgin Mary,
by that most profound humility
by which you deserved to be raised high above
   all the choirs
of Angels and Saints,
I beg of you to intercede for me
that all my sins may be expiated.

Most amiable Virgin Mary,
by that indescribable love
that united you so closely and inseparably to
   God,
I beg of you to intercede for me
that I may obtain an abundance of all merits.

St. Gertrude of Helfta (d. 1334)

In Praise of Mary

O Mary, Mary, temple of the Trinity.
O Mary, bearer of fire.
O Mary, dispenser of mercy.
O Mary, restorer of human generation,
because the world was repurchased
by means of the sustenance
that your flesh found in the Word.
Christ repurchased the world with His Passion,
and you with your suffering of mind and body.

O Mary, peaceful ocean.
O Mary, giver of peace.
O Mary, fruitful land.
You, O Mary, are that new plant
from which we have the fragrant flower
of the Word, Only-begotten Son of God,

because this Word was sown in you,
O fruitful land.
You are the land and the plant.

O Mary, vehicle of fire,
you bore the fire hidden and veiled
beneath the ash of your humanity.

O Mary, vase of humility,
in which there burns the light of true knowl-
    edge
with which you lifted yourself above yourself
and yet were pleasing to the eternal Father;
hence He took and brought you to Himself,
loving you with a singular love.

With this light and fire of your charity
and with the oil of your humility,
you drew and inclined His Divinity to come
    into you—
although He was first drawn to come to us
by the most ardent fire of His inestimable
    charity.

Today, O Mary, you have become a book
in which our rule is written.
In you, today, is written the wisdom
of the eternal Father.
In you, today, is manifested
the strength and freedom of human beings.

I say that
the dignity of human beings is manifested
because when I look at you, O Mary,
I see that the hand of the Holy Spirit

has written the Trinity in you,
forming in you the incarnate Word,
the Only-begotten Son of God.

He has written for us the wisdom of the Father,
that is, the Word.
He has written for us His power,
because He was powerful
in effecting this great mystery.
And He has written for us
the clemency of the Holy Spirit,
because only through grace and the Divine
  clemency
was so great a mystery ordained and accomplished.

But today I ardently make my request,
because it is the day of graces,
and I know that nothing is refused
to you, O Mary.
Today, O Mary, your land has generated
the Savior for us.

O Mary,
blessed are you among women throughout the
  ages!   St. Catherine of Siena (d. 1380)

Prayer of Self-Commendation to Mary

O holy Mary,
my Lady,
into your blessed trust and safe keeping
and into the depths of your mercy
I commend my soul and body this day,

every day of my life,
and at the hour of my death.

To you I entrust
all my hopes and consolations,
all my trials and miseries,
my life and the end of my life.
By your most holy intercession
and by your merits,
may all my actions be directed and disposed
according to your will
and the Will of your Divine Son.

St. Aloysius Gonzaga (d. 1591)

Prayer of Offering to Mary

Most Holy Mary,
Virgin Mother of God,
I am unworthy to be your servant.
Yet moved by your motherly care for me
and longing to serve you,
I choose you this day
to be my Queen, my Advocate, and my Mother.
I firmly resolve ever to be devoted to you
and to do what I can
to encourage others to be devoted to you.

My loving Mother,
through the Precious Blood of your Son shed
     for me,
I beg you to receive me as your servant forever.
Aid me in my actions
and beg for me the grace
never by thought, word, or deed,

to be displeasing in your sight
and that of your most holy Son.
Remember me, dearest Mother,
and do not abandon me at the hour of death.

St. Francis de Sales (d. 1622)

Prayer for the Spirit of Mary

My powerful Queen,
you are all mine through your mercy,
and I am all yours.
Take away from me all that may displease God
and cultivate in me all that is pleasing to Him.

May the light of your faith
dispel the darkness of my mind,
your deep humility
take the place of my pride,
your continual sight of God
fill my memory with His presence.
May the fire of the charity of your heart
inflame the lukewarmness of my own heart.
May your virtues take the place of my sins.
May your merits be my enrichment
and make up for all
that is wanting in me before God.

My beloved Mother,
grant that I may have no other spirit but
your spirit,
to know Jesus Christ and His Divine Will
and to praise and glorify the Lord,
that I may love God with burning love like
yours.

St. Louis de Montfort (d. 1716)

Mary, Our Hope for Salvation

Mary, my Hope,
you are my peace!
Whenever I call upon you or think of you,
I experience such great joy
that my heart is completely ravished.
Whenever some worry troubles me,
it vanishes as soon as I utter your name.
On the sea of the world,
you are the bright star that guides my little
   boat.
And it is under your protection
that I want to live and die . . .

You are my Mother,
for you are the Mother of my God.
What could I fear, O Mary,
if you love me? . . .

You are a Queen that has captured the heart
   of God.
If you wish to save us,
say only that we are your children,
and God will have mercy on us!

St. Alphonsus Liguori (d. 1787)

Mary, Help of Christians

Mary, powerful Virgin,
you are the mighty and glorious protector
of the Church.
You are the marvelous help of Christians.
You are awe-inspiring as an army in battle
   array.

You eliminated heresy in the world.
Amid our anguish, struggle, and distress,
defend us from the power of the enemy,
and at the hour of our death
receive our soul in heaven. St. John Bosco (d. 1888)

Mary, Our Guide to Heaven

Virgin full of grace,
I know that at Nazareth you lived modestly,
without requesting anything more.
Neither ecstasies, nor miracles, nor other
   extraordinary deeds
enhanced your life,
O Queen of the Elect.

The number of the lowly, "the little ones," is
   very great on earth.
They can raise their eyes to you
without any fear.
You are the incomparable Mother
who walks with them along the common way
to guide them to heaven.

Beloved Mother,
in this harsh exile,
I want to live always with you
and follow you every day.
I am enraptured by the contemplation of you
and I discover the depths of the love of your
   Heart.
All my fears vanish under your Motherly gaze,
which teaches me to weep and to rejoice!

St. Theresa of the Child Jesus (d. 1897)

Consecration to Our Lady

Immaculate Virgin,
grant that I may praise you
with my total commitment and my personal
   sacrifice.
Grant that I may live, work, suffer, be consumed, and die for you.

Grant that I may contribute
to an ever greater exaltation of you.
May I render more glory to you
than anyone has every rendered to you in the
   past.
Grant that others may surpass me
in zeal for your exaltation
and that I may in turn surpass them.
Thus, in a noble emulation,
your glory may always increase,
in accord with the desire of the One Who
   exalted you
above all creatures.

In you God is glorified
more than in all His Saints.
Through you God has created the world,
and through you He has called me into existence.

Make me worthy to praise you,
O Immaculate Virgin.

St. Maximilian Kolbe (d. 1941).

Prayers of Popes

Mary Our Refuge

It is sweet music to the ear to say:
I salute you, O Mother!
It is a sweet song to repeat:
I salute you, O holy Mother!

You are my delight, dear hope, and chaste love,
my strength in all adversities.

If my spirit
that is troubled
and stricken by passions
suffers from the painful burden
of sadness and weeping;
if you see your child overwhelmed by misfortune,
O gracious Virgin Mary,
let me find rest in your motherly embrace.

But alas,
already the last day is quickly approaching.
Banish the demon to the infernal depths,
and stay close, dear Mother,
to your aged and erring child.

With a gentle touch,
cover the weary pupils
and kindly consign to God
the soul that is returning to Him.

Leo XIII (d. 1903)

Mary Our Strength

O Virgin, fair as the moon,
delight of the Angels and Saints in heaven,
grant that we may become like you
and that our souls may receive a ray of your
   beauty,
which does not decline with the years
but shines forth into eternity.
O Mary, sun of heaven,
restore life where there is death
and enlighten spirits where there is darkness.
Turn your countenance to your children
and radiate on us your light and your fervor.
O Mary, powerful as an army,
grant victory to our ranks.
We are very weak
and our enemy rages with uttermost conceit.
But under your banner
we are confident of overcoming him. . . .

Save us, O Mary,
fair as the moon,
bright as the sun,
awe-inspiring as an army set in battle array
and sustained not by hatred
but by the ardor of love.

Pius XII (d. 1958)

Recourse to Mary

O Mary,
Your Name is always on my lips and in my
   heart.
From infancy I learned

to love you as my Mother,
to call upon you in dangers,
and to trust in your intercession.
You know my desire to seek truth and do
   good. . . .
O Mary,
sustain me in my will
to live as a faithful disciple of Jesus
so as to build up Christian society
and gladden the holy Catholic Church.
Dear Mother,
I greet you morning and night;
I invoke you along the way;
and from you I await the inspiration and
   consolation
to crown the holy tasks of my earthly vocation,
give glory to God,
and obtain eternal salvation.
O Mary,
in imitation of you at Bethlehem and on
   Calvary,
I too wish to remain always close to Jesus,
the Immortal King of ages and of peoples.

John XXIII (d. 1963)

Mother of the Church

O Mary,
look upon the Church,
look upon the most responsible members
of the Mystical Body of Christ
gathered about you to thank you
and to celebrate you as their Mystical Mother.

O Mary,
bless the great assembly of the hierarchical
   Church,
which also gives birth to brothers and sisters
of Christ,
the firstborn among redeemed humankind.

O Mary,
grant that this Church of Christ—
in defining itself—
will acknowledge you
as its most chosen Mother, Daughter, and
   Sister
as well as its incomparable model,
its glory, its joy, and its hope.

We ask you now
that we may be made worthy of honoring you
because of who you are
and because of what you do
in the wondrous and loving plan of salvation.
Grant that we may praise you,
O holy Virgin! . . .

O Mary,
look upon all humankind,
this modern world in which
the Divine Will calls us to live and work:
It is a world that has turned its back
on the light of Christ;
then it fears and bemoans the frightening
   shadows
that its actions have created on all sides.

May your most human voice,
O most beautiful of virgins,
O most worthy of mothers,
O blessed among women,
invite the world to turn its eyes
toward the life that is the light of human
beings,
toward you who are the precursor-lamp of
Christ,
Who is the sole and the highest Light of the
world.

Implore for the world
the true understanding of its own existence;
implore for the world
the joy of living as the creation of God
and hence the desire and the capacity
to converse—by prayer—with its Maker,
Whose mysterious and blessed image
it reflects within itself.

Implore for the world
the grace to esteem everything as the gift of
God
and hence the virtue to work with generosity
and to make use of such gifts wisely and prov-
idently.

Implore peace for the world.
Fashion brothers and sisters
out of persons who are so divided.
Guide us to a more ordered and peaceful
society.

For those who are suffering—
today there are so many and ever new ones,
afflicted by current misfortunes—
obtain solace;
and for the dead, obtain eternal rest.

Show yourself a Mother to us:
this is our prayer,
O clement, O loving, O sweet Virgin Mary!

Paul VI (d. 1978)

Mary, Mother of All

Mother of the Redeemer,
[in this year dedicated to you,]
with great joy we call you blessed.

In order to carry out His providential plan of
  salvation,
God the Father chose you before the creation
  of the world.
You believed in His love and obeyed His word.

The Son of God desired you for His Mother
when He became man to save the human race.
You received Him with ready obedience and
  undivided heart.
The Holy Spirit loved you as His mystical
  spouse
and He filled you with singular gifts.
You allowed yourself to be led
by His hidden and powerful action.

On the eve of the third Christian Millennium,
we entrust to you the Church

which acknowledges you and invokes you as
   Mother.
On earth you preceded the Church in the pilgrimage of faith:
comfort her in her difficulties and trials,
and make her always the sign and instrument
of intimate union with God
and of the unity of the whole human race.

To you, Mother of Christians,
we entrust in a special way
the peoples who are celebrating
the sixth Centenary or the Millennium
of their acceptance of the Gospel.
Their long history is profoundly marked by
   devotion to you.
Turn toward them your loving glance;
give strength to those who are suffering for the
   faith.

To you, Mother of the human family and of the
   nations,
we confidently entrust the whole of humanity,
with its hopes and fears.
Do not let it lack the light of true wisdom.
Guide its steps in the ways of peace.
Enable all to meet Christ,
the Way and the Truth and the Life.

Sustain us, O Virgin Mary, on our journey of
   faith
and obtain for us the grace of eternal salvation.
O clement, O loving, O sweet Mother of God
and our Mother, Mary!   John Paul II

MARY: MOTHER, QUEEN, AND MEDIATRIX — These are only three of the many titles of Mary. Over the centuries she has been invoked under one or other title by all classes of Christians for all types of requests, and her clients have invariably been heard.

PRAYERS IN HONOR OF MARY'S TITLES

The word "title" has many definitions and uses in English. As used here, it means an appellation of dignity, honor, distinction, or preeminence attached to a person by virtue of rank, office, precedent, privilege, or attainment. In this sense, the titles of Mary are almost endless. The most used Marian title in the Church is "Blessed Virgin Mary." This is how she is named by the Church in official documents.

Offshoots of this Marian title are found in many languages. In English, we speak of "Our Blessed Lady," "Our Blessed Mother," "the Virgin Mary." Other languages speak of the "Holy Virgin," "Most Holy Virgin," and "Holy Mary." Finally, there are the Italian "Madonna" ("My Lady") and the French "Notre Dame" ("Our Lady").

These might be termed Mary's "name" titles. There are also others connected with her "function" (associate of Christ in His Redemption). Some of the more important ones are: Advocate, Associate, Blessed Mother, Daughter of Zion, Exemplar, Handmaid (Servant) of the Lord, Help of Christians, Immaculate Conception, Mediatrix, Mother of the Church, Mother of God, Mother of Mercy, Queen of Peace, and Seat of Wisdom.

Still other titles stem from Mary's relation to certain Christian places, peoples, or religious orders. Some of these are: Our Lady of Fatima, Our Lady of Guadalupe, Our Lady of Lourdes, Our Lady of Good Counsel, Our Lady Help of Christians, and Our Lady of Perpetual Help.

This section offers a selection of prayers to Mary under some of her titles. It helps the faithful to pray to Mary under an aspect or two that they might never have done before. At the same time, it testifies to Mary's universal appeal in the Church.

Traditional Titles

Our Lady of the Blessed Sacrament

See p. 183.

Our Lady of the Cenacle

Most holy Virgin of the Cenacle,
obtain for us the gifts of the Holy Spirit.
May we live in love and perseverance
united in prayer under your guidance and
    teaching
for the greater glory of God.
May we labor both by word and by work
for the salvation of souls
and so deserve to enter everlasting life.

Graciously be near us,
in our present needs,
and comfort us by your power.
By your intercession
may almighty God be pleased to grant us
the favor for which we earnestly pray.

Our Lady, Comforter of the Afflicted

Immaculate Mary, Mother of God,
Comforter of the Afflicted,
accept our humble and confident prayers
and aid us in our spiritual and temporal needs.
Deliver us from all evil,
especially from sin, the greatest evil.
Obtain for us from your Son
every blessing that you see we need,
both in soul and in body,
especially the blessing of Divine grace.

Comfort our souls,
which are troubled and afflicted
amid the many dangers that threaten us
and the countless miseries and misfortunes
that surround us.
Enable us to live a virtuous life,
die a holy death,
and reach eternal happiness in heaven.

Our Lady of Consolation

Mary Immaculate,
our Mother and Consolation,
with confidence I take refuge

in your most loving Heart.
You shall be the dearest object
of my love and veneration.
I shall always have recourse to you
who are the dispenser of the treasures of
    heaven,
that I may have peace in my sorrows,
light in my doubts,
protection in dangers,
and help in all my needs.

Be therefore my refuge, strength, and conso-
    lation,
O Mary the Consoler.
At the hour of my death,
graciously receive the last sighs of my heart
and obtain for me a place in your heavenly
    home,
where all hearts will praise with one accord
the adorable Heart of Jesus
as well as your most lovable Heart forever.
Our tender Mother,
Comforter of the afflicted,
pray for us who have recourse to you.

Our Lady of Divine Providence

See p. 171.

Our Lady of Fatima

See. p. 113.

Our Lady of Good Counsel

Most glorious Virgin,
you were chosen by the eternal Counsel
to be the Mother
of the eternal Word made flesh.
You are the treasurer of Divine graces
and the advocate of sinners.
I who am your most unworthy servant
have recourse to you.
Graciously be my guide and counselor
in this valley of tears.

Obtain for me,
through the Precious Blood of your Divine Son,
the forgiveness of my sins,
the salvation of my soul,
and the means necessary to obtain it.
In like manner, obtain for holy Church
victory over her enemies
and the spread of Jesus' Kingdom
over the whole earth.

Our Lady of Guadalupe

See p. 160.

Our Lady, Help of Christians

See p. 72.

Our Lady of the Immaculate Conception

See p. 159.

Our Lady of La Salette

Our Lady of La Salette,
true Mother of Sorrows,
remember the tears that you shed on Calvary.
Remember, also, the care that you take
to shield me from the justice of God.
Do not now abandon your child,
for whom you have done so much.

Inspired with this consoling thought,
I cast myself at your feet,
in spite of my unfaithfulness and ingratitude.
Do not reject my prayer,
O reconciling Virgin.
Convert me;
obtain for me the grace to love Jesus
above all things
and to console you by a holy life,
so that one day I may see you in heaven.

Our Lady of Lourdes

See p. 151.

Our Lady, Mediatrix of Graces

Most holy Mary,
great Queen of heaven,
the very treasure of life
and ever-flowing channel of Divine grace!
By the ineffable virtues
infused into your soul
at your Immaculate Conception,

you were so pleasing in God's sight
that you were privileged
to conceive in your virginal womb
the very Author of life and of grace,
Jesus Christ, our Lord.
By becoming the Mother of the God-Man,
you also became the Mother of redeemed
  humankind.

Mother of grace and life,
of mercy and forgiveness,
turn to me your kind face.
Behold my many miseries of body and soul.
Raise me up to a state
of perfect friendship with God.
Obtain for me
the grace of final perseverance.

Our Lady, Mother of Mercy

Hail, most gracious Mother of Mercy,
through whom we obtain forgiveness!
Who would not love you?
You are our light in uncertainty,
our comfort in sorrow,
our consolation in trial,
our refuge from every danger and temptation.
You are our sure hope of salvation,
second only to your only-begotten Son.

Happy are they who love you,
our Lady!
I beg you to listen to my prayers,
even though I am a poor sinner.

Scatter the darkness of my sins
by the bright beams of your holiness
so that I may be pleasing to you.

Mother of Good Hope

Mary Immaculate,
the precious name of Mother of Good Hope,
with which we honor you,
fills our hearts to overflowing
with the sweetest consolation
and moves us to hope for every blessing from
you.

If such a title has been given to you,
it is a sure sign
that no one has recourse to you in vain.

Therefore, with a mother's love
accept our devout homage,
as we earnestly beg you
to be gracious to us in our every need.

Above all, we beg you to make us live
in constant union with you
and your Divine Son Jesus on earth
so that we may deserve
to be with you in heaven.

Our Lady of Mount Carmel

See p. 153.

Our Lady of Perpetual Help

O Mother of Perpetual Help,
grant that I may ever invoke your powerful
    name,
which is the safeguard of the living
and the salvation of the dying.
O pure Virgin Mary,
let your name be henceforth ever on my lips.
Whenever I call on you by name,
hasten to help me.
When I speak your sacred name
or even think of you,
what consolation and confidence,
what sweetness and emotion fill my soul!

I thank God
for having given you
so sweet, powerful, and lovely a name
for my good.
Let my love for you prompt me ever to greet
    you
as Mother of Perpetual Help.

Our Lady, Queen of Peace

Most holy Virgin,
by your Divine Motherhood you merited
to share in your Divine Son's prerogative of
    universal Kingship,
and to be called Queen of Peace.
May your powerful intercession guard your
    people

from all hatred and discord among themselves
and direct their hearts in the way of peace.
Your Son came to teach us this way
for the good and well-being of all,
and your Church continues to guide our steps
along that same way.

Look kindly upon the efforts of Christ's Vicar
to call together and unite nations
around the only center of saving faith.
Enlighten the rulers of our country
and of all countries on earth
to follow this path to peace.
Grant that there may be peace
in our hearts,
in our families,
and in our world.

Our Lady of the Rosary

See p. 158.

Our Lady of the Sacred Heart

O Lady of the Sacred Heart,
remember what ineffable power
your Divine Son has given you
over His own adorable Heart.
You are the heavenly Treasurer of the Heart
that is the limitless source of all graces.
You are free to open it to us
at your good pleasure
in order to pour out upon humankind
 the riches of love and mercy,

light and salvation,
that are contained in it.
Graciously hear our prayers
and grant the request we now make
(mention your request).

Our Lady of Sorrows

See pp. 157, 184.

Contemporary Titles

Our Lady, Associate of the Redeemer

Blessed are you, O Mary,
Virgin Mother of Christ
and the generous Associate of our Redeemer.
You conceived, bore, and nourished Christ,
you presented Him to the Father in the Temple,
and you were united with Him in His work,
especially in His Death on the Cross.
You thus cooperated,
by your obedience, faith, hope, and love,
in the work of the Savior
in giving back supernatural life to souls.

Help us to share in the Redemption
by uniting our sufferings to those of Christ.
Grant that we may even rejoice in them,
so that we may be filled with joy
when He comes again in glory.

Our Lady, Daughter of Zion

Blessed are you, O Mary,
Daughter of Zion.
You were chosen by God
as the crown of Israel
and the beginning of the Church
to reveal to all peoples
that salvation is born from Israel
and that the new family of God
springs from a chosen root.

By nature, you are the daughter of Adam
who by your sinlessness undid Eve's sin.
By faith you are the true child of Abraham
who first believed and so conceived.
By descent you are the branch
from the root of Jesse,
bearing the flower that is Jesus.

Obtain for us
to follow your example
by offering you the homage of our heartfelt faith
and placing in you alone our hope of salvation.

Our Lady, Handmaid of the Lord

Blessed are you, O Mary,
Handmaid of the Lord.
You welcomed the Angel's announcement
and became the Mother of the Word.
In the silence of your Heart,
you meditated on the heavenly words
and became a disciple of the Divine Master.

Open our hearts
to the blessedness of listening.
By the power of the Holy Spirit,
may we too become a holy place
in which the Word of salvation
is fulfilled today.

Our Lady, Mother of the Church

See p. 77.

Our Lady, Mother of Reconciliation

Blessed are you, O Mary,
Mother of Reconciliation.
Although you were sinless,
God gave you
a Heart of compassion for sinners
in order to call them back to His love.

Teach us to see your love as our Mother
and turn to you with trust
as we ask forgiveness from God.
Make us contemplate your beauty of spirit
and seek to turn away from sin in its ugliness.
Help us to take your words and example to heart
and learn to keep your Son's commandments.

Our Lady, Mother and Teacher

Blessed are you, O Mary,
Mother and Teacher in the Spirit.
You are a Teacher
who keeps the words of the Lord
in her heart.

You are a Mother
who gently invites us to go up
to the mountain of the Lord,
which is Christ Himself.

As our Teacher,
instruct us in the fear of God,
to live by the spirit of the Gospel,
to look up to you in prayer,
to love God above all things,
to be rapt in contemplation of His Word,
and to serve the needs of others.
As our Mother,
watch over us
and keep us under your protection.
Make us imitate your virtues
and reach our heavenly home with you.

Our Lady, the New Woman

Blessed are you, O Mary,
the New Woman.
Conceived without stain of sin
and enriched by gifts of grace,
you are the new Eve,
associated with Jesus, the New Adam,
as His Mother and Companion.
By your faith and obedience,
you undid the loss inflicted on humankind
by the unfaithfulness and disobedience
of the first Eve.

Help us to emulate
the active and responsible consent

that you gave in dialogue with God.
Teach us to make courageous choices
as you did in choosing the state of virginity.
Give us a love for the poor and lowly
in accord with your life and sentiments
as expressed in the *Magnificat* Prayer.

Our Lady, Queen of the Universe

Blessed are you, O Mary,
Queen of the universe.
You are gloriously reigning in heaven
because you were the lowly handmaid on earth.
You are our Queen and Mother
because you became the Mother
of the Messianic King.
You are the Queen who intercedes for us
with her Son
as our Advocate of grace.
You are the Queen
who is the sign of the Church in future glory,
because what was accomplished in you
will be accomplished in all members
of Christ's Mystical Body.

As your Queenship is one of love and service
rather than pomp and power,
teach us to adhere to God's plan
and be dedicated to your Son Jesus.
Help us to deny ourselves in order to gain
the souls of our brothers and sisters.
Let us follow the modest things on earth
and reach the heights of heaven.

DEVOTIONS TO MARY — CENTERED ON THE ROSARY—Among the many devotions that Catholics practice in honor of Mary is the devotion of the Holy Rosary. The Church has enriched it with indulgences and exhorts her members to make frequent use of it.

PRAYERS FROM NOVENAS AND DEVOTIONS

We have already seen many prayers to the Blessed Virgin Mary. This section is concerned with some of the more popular devotions to our Lady. These have been time-tested and found to be very powerful means of keeping Catholics close to Mary and her Divine Son.

The outstanding devotion is the Rosary. The Scriptural riches of this devotion are of permanent value. After a short lapse into disuse, the Rosary has made a stirring comeback in our day. And in the eyes of the dedicated follower of Mary it is still the devotion par excellence.

Another Marian devotion is the Novena to Our Lady of the Miraculous Medal, which is the outgrowth of Mary's appearances to St. Bernadette at Lourdes. It has been a favorite with Catholics since then and can still be used with the necessary updating as found herein.

The appearances of Mary to the three children of Fatima provided the impetus for another devotion—the First Saturdays. Those devoted to Mary cultivate this practice, which fosters devotion to Our Lady of the Rosary.

The assigning of months to Mary (October to the Rosary and May to our Lady herself) encourages the faithful to perform these devotions in honor of Mary. The Church desires that Mary be honored in liturgical but also in non-liturgical devotions, which may in reality be more familiar to and better appreciated by them. So long as the latter follow the recommendations of Vatican II, they are perfectly proper and should be used with frequency by all Catholics.

The devotions found herein were selected over many others primarily because of their popularity but also because they constitute perfect exemplars for other devotions to the Blessed Virgin.

The Holy Rosary

The devotion of the Holy Rosary has been treasured in the Church for centuries. It is a summary of Christian faith in language and prayers inspired by the Bible. It calls to mind the most important events in the lives of Jesus and Mary. These events are called Mysteries and are divided into four groups of decades. They are: the five Joyful, the five Luminous, the five Sorrowful, and the five Glorious Mysteries. Each decade consists of one "Our Father," ten "Hail Marys," and one "Glory Be to the Father."

How to Say the Rosary

1. *Begin on the crucifix and say the Apostles' Creed.*
2. *On the 1st bead, say 1 Our Father.*
3. *On the next 3 beads, say Hail Mary.*
4. *Next say 1 Glory Be. Then announce and think of the first Mystery and say 1 our Father.*
5. *Say 10 Hail Marys and 1 Glory Be to the Father.*

6. *Announce the second Mystery and continue in the same way until each of the five Mysteries of the selected group or decades is said.*

The Five Joyful Mysteries

(Said on Mondays, and Saturdays, and Sundays from Advent until Lent)

The Joyful Mysteries direct our mind to the Son of God, Jesus Christ, our Lord and Savior, Who took human nature from a human mother, Mary. They also bring to our attention some of the extraordinary events that preceded, accompanied, and followed Christ's Birth.

1. The Annunciation

Lk 1 26-38; Isa 7:10-15

Mary, you received with deep humility
the news of the Angel Gabriel
that you were to be the Mother of God's Son;
obtain for me a similar *humility*.

2. The Visitation

Lk 1:39-56

Mary, you showed true charity in visiting
Elizabeth
and remaining with her for three months
before the birth of John the Baptist;
obtain for me the grace to *love my neighbor*.

3. The Birth of Jesus

Lk 2:1-14; Mt 2:1-12; Gal 4:1-7

Jesus, You lovingly accepted poverty
when You were placed in the manger in the
stable

although You were our God and Redeemer;
grant that I may have the *spirit of poverty.*

4. The Presentation in the Temple

Lk 2:22-40

Mary, you obeyed the law of God
in presenting the Child Jesus in the Temple;
obtain for me the *virtue of obedience.*

5. The Finding in the Temple

Lk 2:42-52

Mary, you were filled with sorrow at the loss
  of Jesus
and overwhelmed with joy on finding Him
surrounded by Teachers in the Temple;
obtain for me the *virtue of piety.*

The Five Luminous Mysteries*

(Said on Thursdays [except during Lent])

*The Luminous Mysteries recall to our mind important
events of the Public Ministry of Christ through which He
announces the coming of the Kingdom of God, bears witness to it in His works, and proclaims its demands—
showing that the Mystery of Christ is most evidently a
Mystery of Light.*

1. Christ's Baptism in the Jordan

Mt 3:13-17; Is 42:1-2, 4-5

Jesus, at Your Baptism in the Jordan,
the Father called You His beloved Son

---

* Added to the Mysteries of the Rosary by Pope John Paul II in his Apostolic
Letter of October 16, 2002, entitled *The Rosary of the Virgin Mary.* They are
reprinted here from our book *Pray the Rosary*, which in 2002 received the
Imprimatur from Most Rev. Frank J. Rodimer, Bishop of Paterson.

and the Holy Spirit descended upon You
to invest You with Your mission;
help me to *keep my Baptismal Promises.*

2. Christ's Self-Manifestation
at the Wedding in Cana

Jn 2:1-11

Mary, the first among believers in Christ,
as a result of your intercession at Cana,
your Son changed water into wine
and opened the hearts of the disciples to
faith;
obtain for me the grace to *do whatever Jesus
says.*

3. Christ's Proclamation of
the Kingdom of God

Mk 1:15; Mt 5:1-11

Jesus, You preached the Kingdom of God
with its call to forgiveness,
inaugurating the ministry of mercy,
which You continue to exercise,
especially through the Sacrament of Reconciliation;
help me to *seek forgiveness for my sins.*

4. The Transfiguration of Our Lord

Mt 17:1-8; Mk 9:2-8; Lk 9:28-36

Jesus, at Your Transfiguration,
the glory of the Godhead shone forth from
Your face

as the Father commanded the Apostles to
  hear You
and be transfigured by the Holy Spirit;
help me to *be a new person in You.*

5. Christ's Institution of the Eucharist

Mt 26:26-30; 1 Cor 11:23-25

Jesus, at the Last Supper, You instituted the
  Eucharist,
offering Your Body and Blood as food
under the signs of bread and wine
and testifying to Your love for humanity;
help me to *attain active participation at Mass.*

The Five Sorrowful Mysteries

*(Said on Tuesdays and Fridays throughout the year,
and daily from Ash Wednesday until Easter Sunday)*

*The Sorrowful Mysteries recall to our mind the mysterious
events surrounding Christ's sacrifice of His life in order that
sinful humanity might be reconciled with God.*

1. The Agony in the Garden

Mt 26:36-40

Jesus, in the Garden of Gethsemane,
You suffered a bitter agony because of our sins;
grant me *true contrition.*

2. The Scourging at the Pillar

Mt 27:24-26; 1 Pet 2:21-25

Jesus, You endured a cruel scourging
and Your flesh was torn by heavy blows;
help me to have the *virtue of purity.*

3. The Crowning with Thorns
Mt 27:27-31

Jesus, You patiently endured the pain
from the crown of sharp thorns
that was forced upon Your head;
grant me the strength to have *moral courage.*

4. The Carrying of the Cross
Mt 27:32

Jesus, You willingly carried Your Cross
for love of Your Father and all people;
grant me the *virtue of patience.*

5. The Crucifixion
Mt 27:33-50; Jn 19:31-37

Jesus, for love of me
You endured three hours of torture on the
    Cross
and gave up Your spirit;
grant me the grace of *final perseverance.*

The Five Glorious Mysteries

*(Said on Wednesdays [except during Lent] and the
Sundays from Easter until Advent)*

*The Glorious Mysteries recall to our mind the ratification of
Christ's sacrifice for the redemption of the world, and our sharing in the fruits of His sacrifice.*

1. The Resurrection
Mk 16:1-7; Jn 20:19-31

Jesus, You rose from the dead in triumph
and remained for forty days with Your disci-
    ples,

instructing and encouraging them;
increase my *faith*.

2. The Ascension
Mk 16:14-20; Acts 1:1-11

Jesus, in the presence of Mary and the disciples
You ascended to heaven
to sit at the Father's right hand;
increase the *virtue of hope* in me.

3. The Descent of the Holy Spirit
Jn 14:23-31; Acts 2:1-11

Jesus, in fulfillment of Your promise
You sent the Holy Spirit upon Mary and the disciples
under the form of tongues of fire;
increase my *love for God.*

4. The Assumption
Lk 1:41-50; Ps 45; Gen 3:15

Mary by the power of God you were assumed into heaven
and united with your Divine Son;
help me to have *true devotion to you.*

5. The Crowning of the Blessed Virgin
Rev 12:1; Jud 13:18-20; 15:9-10

Mary, you were crowned Queen of heaven
by your Divine Son
to the great joy of all the Saints;
obtain *eternal happiness* for me.

At the end of the Rosary, one may add the prayer "Hail, Holy Queen," p. 12, and the following prayer:

Prayer after the Rosary

O God,
Whose only-begotten Son,
by His Life, Death, and Resurrection,
has purchased for us the rewards of eternal
  life;
grant, we beseech You, that,
meditating upon these Mysteries
of the Most Holy Rosary of the Blessed
  Virgin Mary,
we may imitate what they contain
and obtain what they promise,
through the same Christ our Lord.

The Litany of Loreto, p. 17, may also be said.

Novena in Honor of Our Lady of the Miraculous Medal

The medal of the Immaculate Conception, known as the Miraculous Medal, was revealed by Mary herself to St. Catherine Labouré in 1830. It bears the words: "O Mary, conceived without sin, pray for us who have recourse to you." Through it and through this Novena many graces have been obtained by Mary for her clients.

Invocation

O Mary, conceived without sin.
—Pray for us who have recourse to you.

Hymn

Immaculate Mary, your praises we sing.
You reign now in splendor with Jesus, our
  King.

Ave, Ave, Ave Maria,
Ave, Ave Maria.

In heaven the blessed your glory proclaim,
On earth we your children invoke your fair
    name.

We pray for the Church, our true Mother on
    earth.
And we beg you to watch over the land of
    our birth.
We pray you, O Mother, may God's Will be
    done;
We pray for His glory, may His Kingdom
    come.

Reading

Jud 13:18-19; 15:9

Blessed are you, daughter,
by the Most High God,
above all the other women on earth.
And blessed be the Lord God,
the Creator of heaven and earth.
The hope that inspired you will never fade
from the memory of those who praise the
    power of God.
You are the glory of Jerusalem,
the surpassing pride of Israel,
the great honor of our people.

In your splendor and your beauty,
—triumph and reign, O Virgin Mary.

Intercessions

My brothers and sisters,
let us say to our Savior
Who willed to be born of the Virgin Mary:
℟. *Lord, may Your Mother intercede for us!*

Jesus, while hanging on the Cross,
You gave Your Mother to be the Mother of
John;
—help us live as her sons.

Savior, Your Mother stood by the Cross;
—through her intercession,
help us welcome a share in Your sufferings.

Word eternal, You elected Mary
to be the incorruptible ark of Your presence,
—free us from the corruption of sin.

Son of Justice, grant us in the immaculate
Virgin,
a guiding light of return to You,
—that we may always walk in Your light.

Lord, enable us to imitate Mary Your Mother
who chose the better portion,
—by seeking the food that remains to life
eternal.

King of kings, You willed Your Mother
to be assumed into heaven with You in body
and soul;
—may we always attend to what comes from
above.

Lord of heaven and earth,

You made Mary Queen at Your right hand,
—help us attain a share in the same glory.

Savior of the world, through Your redemptive
    power
You preserved Your Mother from all stain;
—save us from sin.

Redeemer, You had Mary as the purest dwell-
    ing-place for Your presence,
and You made her the holy vehicle of the Spirit;
—make us lasting temples of Your Spirit.

Novena Prayer

O Immaculate Virgin Mary,
Mother of our Lord Jesus and our Mother,
penetrated with the most lively confidence,
in your all-powerful and never-failing inter-
    cession,
manifested so often through the Miraculous
    Medal,
we your loving and trustful children,
implore you to obtain for us the graces and
    favors
we ask during this Novena,
if they be beneficial to our immortal souls,
and the souls for whom we pray.
(Here privately mention your petitions.)

You know, O Mary, how often our souls have
    been
the sanctuaries of your Son, Who hates
    iniquity.
Obtain for us a deep hatred of sin,

and that purity of heart which will attach us
to God alone,
so that our every thought, word, and deed
may tend to His greater glory.
Obtain for us also a spirit of prayer and self-
denial,
that we may recover by penance
what we have lost by sin,
and at length attain to that blessed abode
where you are the Queen of Angels and all
people.

Concluding Prayer

Father,
through the Immaculate Conception of the
Virgin
You prepared a worthy place for Your Son.
In view of the foreseen Death of Your Son
You preserved her from all sin.
Through her intercession
grant that we may also reach You with clean
hearts.
We ask this in the name of Jesus the Lord.

May Devotions

Invocation

You are all pure, O Mary.
—And there is in you no stain of sin.

Reading

Song 2:10-13

Arise, my beloved, my fair one,
and come!

For see, the winter is past,
the rains are over and gone.
The flowers appear in the countryside;
the season of joyful songs has arrived,
and the voice of the turtle dove is heard in
   our land.
The fig tree puts forth its figs,
and the blossoms on the vine give forth their
   fragrance.
Arise, my beloved, my fair one,
and come!

Blessed are you, O Mary.
—For the world's salvation came forth from
   you.

Intercessions

Let us implore Mary our Mother for faith
—to walk along the path of righteousness all
   our lives.
Hail Mary . . .

Let us implore Mary our Mother for the consoling hope
—that enables us to work in this world
but also keep our eyes fixed on the next.
Hail Mary . . .

Let us implore Mary our Mother for the
   virtue of love,
—which is the bond of perfection, unity, and
   glory.
Hail Mary . . .

Let us offer Mary our Mother the flower
of our love, joy, purity, and hope
—that her joy may be full.

Prayer

Heavenly Father,
You chose the Blessed Virgin Mary
to be the Mother of Your only Son, Jesus Christ.
Through her intercession
grant us the grace to attain the glory of heaven.
We ask this in the name of Jesus the Lord.

The Five First Saturdays in Honor of the Immaculate Heart of Mary

Mary's Great Promise at Fatima

The observance of the First Saturday in honor of the Immaculate Heart of Mary is intended to console her Immaculate Heart and to make reparation to it for all the blasphemies and ingratitude of human beings.

This devotion and the wonderful promises connected with it were revealed by the Blessed Virgin with these words recorded by Lucy, one of the three children to whom the Blessed Virgin appeared at Fatima, Portugal, in 1917:

I promise to help at the hour of death, with the graces needed for salvation, whoever on the First Saturday of five consecutive months shall:

1. *Confess and receive Holy Communion.*
2. *Recite five decades of the Rosary.*
3. *And keep me company for fifteen minutes while meditating on the [twenty] Mysteries of the Rosary, with the intention of making reparation to me.*

Act of Reparation

O most holy Virgin and our Mother,
we listen with grief to the complaints
of your Immaculate Heart surrounded with
   the thorns
placed therein at every moment
by the blasphemies and ingratitude
of ungrateful humanity.
We are moved by the ardent desire
of loving you as our Mother
and of promoting a true devotion
to your Immaculate Heart.

We therefore kneel before you
to manifest the sorrow we feel for the grievances
that people cause you,
and to atone by our prayers and sacrifices
for the offenses with which they return your love.
Obtain for them and for us the pardon of so
   many sins.
Hasten the conversion of sinners
that they may love Jesus
and cease to offend the Lord, already so much
   offended,
and will not fall into hell.
Turn your eyes of mercy toward us,
that we may love God with all our heart on earth
and enjoy Him forever in heaven.

Novena Prayer to the Mother of God
(January 1)

I greet you, ever-blessed Virgin,
Mother of God and miracle of almighty power!

I greet you,
sanctuary of the Most Holy Trinity
and Queen of the Universe.
Mother of Mercy and Refuge of Sinners,
attracted by your beauty and sweetness
as well as by your tender compassion,
I confidently turn to you,
miserable as I am,
and beg you to obtain for me
of your dear Son
the favor I request in this Novena:
(mention your request).
Above all, I beg you
to be my Mother and Patroness,
to receive me into the number of your devoted
    children,
and to guide me from your high throne of
    glory.

Novena Prayer to Our Lady of Lourdes
(February 11)

Ever Immaculate Virgin,
by appearing in the Grotto of Lourdes,
you were pleased to make it a privileged
    sanctuary,
from which you dispense your favors;
and already many sufferers have obtained
the cure of their infirmities,
both spiritual and corporal.

Through your loving compassion
shown to thousands of pilgrims who come to
    Lourdes,

and through your special love
for your devoted client Bernadette,
I ask for this grace if it be the Will of God:
(mention your request).

Out of gratitude for your favors,
I will endeavor to imitate your virtues
that I may one day share your glory.

Novena Prayer to Our Lady of Sorrows
(September 15)

Most holy and afflicted Virgin,
Mother of Sorrows and Queen of Martyrs,
you stood motionless at the foot of the Cross
beneath your dying Son.
Through the sword of grief that pierced you,
the unceasing suffering of your life of sorrow,
and the bliss that now fully repays you
for your past trials and afflictions,
look upon me with a Mother's tenderness
as I pray before you to venerate your sorrows
and place my request
in the sanctuary of your wounded Heart.

I beg you to present to Jesus,
in union with the infinite merits of His Passion
    and Death,
your sufferings at the foot of the Cross,
and through the power of both,
to grant my request:
(mention your request).
Refuge of sinners and hope of all humankind,
accept my petition and grant it,
if it be according to the Will of God.

Novena Prayer to Our Lady of Guadalupe
(December 12)

Our Lady of Guadalupe,
according to your message in Mexico,
I venerate you as "the Virgin Mother
of the true God for Whom we live,
the Creator of all the world,
Maker of heaven and earth."
In spirit, I kneel before your most holy Image,
which you miraculously imprinted upon the
  cloak
of the Indian Juan Diego.

With the faith of the countless pilgrims
who visit your shrine,
I beg of you this favor:
(mention your request).
Our Lady of Guadalupe,
I beg you to grant my request,
if it is the Will of God,
in order that I may bear witness
to your love, compassion, help, and protection.

The Thirty Days' Prayer to the Blessed Virgin Mary

Ever glorious and blessed Mary,
Queen of Virgins,
Mother of Mercy,
and Hope of dejected and desolate souls,
through the sword of sorrow
that pierced your Heart

while your only Son Jesus, our Lord,
suffered death and ignominy on the Cross
and through that filial love He had for you,
grieving in your grief,
while He entrusted you to St. John,
I beg you:
take pity on my poverty and necessities,
have compassion on my anxieties and cares,
assist and comfort me in all my infirmities and
   miseries.
You are the sweet Consolatrix and Refuge
of the needy and the afflicted;
hear my prayer.

In just punishment for my sins,
I am encompassed with evils
and oppressed with anguish of spirit.
To whom can I flee for more secure shelter,
O loving Mother of my Lord and Savior,
except to your Motherly protection?
Listen, then, to my humble and earnest re-
   quest.

I ask it
through the infinite mercy of your dear Son,
through that love and condescension
with which He embraced our nature
when in compliance with the Divine Will
you consented to conceive
and nine months later brought Him forth
to visit this world and bless it with His presence.

I ask it through that anguish of mind
with which your beloved Son was overwhelmed

in the Garden
when He besought His eternal Father
to remove from Him,
if possible, the bitter chalice of His Passion.

I ask it
through the threefold repetition of His prayer
in the Garden,
from which you afterward accompanied Him
   in sorrow
to the doleful theater of His Sufferings and
   Death.

I ask it
through the welts and sores of His virginal
   flesh,
occasioned by the cords and whips
with which He was bound and scourged,
when stripped of His seamless garment,
for which His executioners afterward cast lots.

I ask it
through the scoffs and ignominies
by which He was insulted,
the false accusations and unjust sentence
by which He was condemned to death,
and which He bore with heavenly patience.

I ask it
through His bitter tears and bloody sweat,
His silence and resignation,
His sadness and grief of Heart.

I ask it
through the Blood that trickled
from His royal and sacred Head
when struck with a scepter of a reed
and pierced with the crown of thorns.

I ask it
through the excruciating torments He suffered
when His Hands and Feet were fastened with
nails
to the tree of the Cross.

I ask it
through His vehement thirst
and the bitter potion of vinegar and gall.

I ask it
through His dereliction on the Cross
when He exclaimed:
"My God, My God, why have You forsaken
Me?"

I ask it
through His mercy extended to the good thief
and through His recommending His precious
Soul and Spirit
into the hands of His eternal Father
before He expired, saying:
"It is consummated."

I ask it
through the Blood mixed with water,
which issued from His sacred Side,
when pierced with a lance
and from which a flood of grace has flowed to us.

I ask it
through His immaculate Life, bitter Passion,
and ignominious Death on the Cross
at which Nature itself was thrown into convul-
sions
by the bursting of rocks,
the rending of the Temple veil,
the earthquake,
and the darkening of the sun and moon.

I ask it
through His Descent into hell,
where He comforted the Saints of the Old Law
with His presence
and led captivity captive.

I ask it
through His glorious victory over death
when He rose again to life on the third day
and through the joy
that His appearance for forty days afterward
gave you and His Apostles and disciples
when He miraculously ascended into heaven
in your presence.

I ask it
through the grace of the Holy Spirit,
infused into the hearts of the disciples,
when He descended upon them
in the form of fiery tongues
and by which they were inspired with zeal
in the conversion of the world
when they went to preach the Gospel.

I ask it
through the awesome appearance of your Son at
the last day,
when He shall come to judge the living and the
dead.

I ask it
through the compassion He bore you in this life
and the ineffable joy you felt
at your Assumption into heaven,
where you are eternally absorbed
in the sweet contemplation
of His Divine perfections.

O glorious and ever-blessed Virgin,
comfort the heart of your suppliant,
by obtaining for me the grant of the intentions
that I now earnestly solicit.
(Here mention your request.)
Since I firmly believe
that my Divine Savior honors you as His beloved Mother,
to whom He can refuse nothing,
let me speedily experience the efficacy
of your powerful intercession
according to the tenderness of your Motherly
affection
and according to His filial, loving Heart,
which mercifully grants the requests
and complies with the desires
of those who love and fear Him.

O most blessed Virgin,
obtain for me also from your dear Son,

our Lord and God,
a lively faith, firm hope, perfect love,
true contrition of heart,
unfeigned tears of compunction,
sincere confession,
condign satisfaction,
abstinence from sin,
love of God and neighbor,
patient bearing of affronts and ignominies,
and an opprobrious death itself
out of love for your Son,
our Savior Jesus Christ.

O sacred Mother of God,
also obtain for me
perseverance in good works,
performance of good resolutions,
mortifications of self-will,
a pious conversation through life,
and at my last moments
strong and sincere repentance
accompanied by such a lively and attentive pres-
    ence of mind
as may enable me to receive
the Last Sacraments of the Church worthily
and to die in your friendship and favor.

Finally, I beg you,
obtain life everlasting for the souls
of my parents, my brothers and sisters,
and my relatives and benefactors,
living or dead.

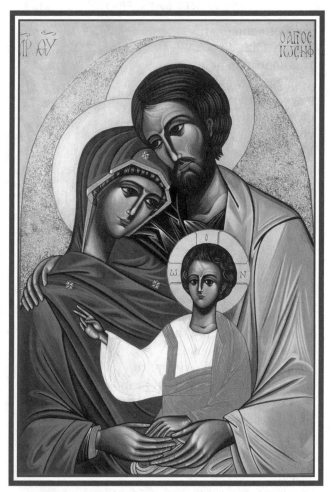

MARY'S INTERCESSION AT CANA—At the wedding feast of Cana, Jesus performed His first miracle through Mary's intercession. We make use of general prayers to ask Mary (and through her, Jesus) to help us in all our needs.

124

PRAYERS FOR VARIOUS NEEDS

The great devotee of Mary in the 12th century, St. Bernard of Clairvaux, had these beautiful words to say about having devotion to Mary and praying to her:

"In danger, anguish, or doubt,
    think of Mary and call upon her.
Let the name of Mary
    never be far from your lips or heart.
And to obtain the fruit of her prayers,
    do not forget the example of her life.
Following Mary,
    you will never lose your way.
Praying to her,
    you will never sink into despair.
Contemplating Mary,
    you will never go wrong.
With Mary's support,
    you will never fall.
Beneath her protection,
    you will never fear.
Under her guidance,
    you will never tire.
And with her help,
    you will reach your heavenly goal."

This section puts at the disposal of everyone prayers to Mary for various needs. In doing so, it offers models for praying to Mary in our own words. The prayers are for both material and spiritual needs. They testify to the truth of the words of the great French Catholic writer Charles Peguy:

"The prayers to the Blessed Virgin are prayers of reserve for times, when we do not succeed in praying any other way. There is not even one such prayer that the most wretched sinner cannot say in all truth. Indeed, in the plan of salvation, prayer to Mary is the ultimate recourse; with it we can never be lost."

Abandonment to Mary

Virgin full of goodness,
I entrust my life to you.
If you will not help me, where can I turn?
But all the Saints have said
that you help all your children who go to you,
even the worst sinner.
I pray for myself and all sinners.
I pray for the souls in purgatory.
May your beautiful Motherly care always be
   with me.
May I be humble as you were humble.
Pride blocks the heart,
and Jesus cannot come in.
May you, O Mother, ever be my model
in humility and resignation to the Will of God.

For My Birthday

Mary, my Mother,
today is the anniversary of my birth,
the day on which the heavenly Father
allowed me to enter this wonderful world.

Help me to realize that I was put here for a
    reason:
to know, love, and serve God on earth
and be happy forever with Him in heaven.
Teach me the fleetingness of time
and the enduring length of eternity.
Keep me close to you until my death,
starting from today,
which is the first day of the rest of my life.

For My Children

Mary, Mother of God,
and Mother of all Christians,
you presented your Divine Son in the
    Temple.
Now I present to you the children
whom God has graciously given me.
By the grace of their Baptism,
which incorporated them into Christ,
you became their Mother.
I entrust them to you,
to your guidance and vigilance.

Make them healthy in both soul and body.
Help them to become useful citizens
of their own country,
but let them not forget
the Kingdom of God.
If they go astray,
lead them back to your Son
so that they may obtain forgiveness and peace.
Enable us all to reach eternal happiness
with you and your Divine Son in heaven.

For My Parents

Mary, my Mother,
you brought Jesus into this world
and looked after Him
as my parents brought me into this world
and look after my spiritual and material
  health.
Obtain for them God's choicest blessings
and enrich their souls with grace.
Keep them close to you all their lives
and lead them to Jesus.

May I and their other children be ever
their joy in this life
and their crown of glory in the next.
Bring them to a ripe old age
in health of mind and body
and grant them a holy death
in union with you and your Divine Son.

For a Happy Death

Jesus, Mary, and Joseph,
I give you my heart and my soul.

Jesus, Mary, and Joseph,
assist me in my last agony.

Jesus, Mary, and Joseph,
may I breathe forth my soul in peace with you
in my last agony.

Dedication of a Family to Mary

Most Blessed Virgin Mary,
I kneel here before you with my family
and choose you
for my Lady, Mother, and Advocate with God.
I dedicate myself and all who belong to me
to your service forever.
Take us under your protection.
Help us in life and at the hour of our death.

Bless me and all my family.
Never let any of us offend your Son.
In every temptation defend us.
Protect us in every danger.
Provide for us in the necessities of life.
Comfort us in every sorrow, in every sickness,
and especially in the final sorrow of death.
Grant that we may all enter into heaven
to thank you and, in your company,
to praise and love Jesus our Redeemer
for all eternity.

To Attain Eternal Life

Mother of Christ,
I appeal to your mercy
and beg you to pray to your Divine Son for me.
Let me share in the benefits of His sacrifice
that I may be truly sorry for my sins
and save my soul.
I want to belong to His Kingdom.

Help me to live up to the teaching of His
    Church,

which He founded for the salvation of all.
Through you we received the Author of Life;
through you may we reach eternal life.

For an Expectant Mother

Mary,
most pure Virgin and Mother of God,
I remind you of the blessed moment
when for the first time
you saw your newborn Child
and enfolded Him in your arms.
Through this joy of your Motherly Heart,
obtain for me the grace
that I and my child may be protected
from all danger.

Mary,
Mother of my Savior,
I remind you of the unspeakable joy you felt
when, after three days of painful seeking,
you again found your Divine Son.
Through this joy,
obtain for me the grace
to bring into the world
a healthy and well-formed child.

Most glorious Virgin Mary,
I remind you of the heavenly joy
that flooded your Motherly Heart
when your Son appeared to you after His Res-
    surrection.
Through this great joy,
obtain for my child

the blessings of holy Baptism,
so that my child may be admitted to the
   Church,
the Mystical Body of your Divine Son.

For My Friends

Dear Mother Mary,
on earth your Son had many close friends.
In this way He showed
that friendship is one of life's greatest
   blessings.
Help me to appreciate the friends God has
   given me
to love me in spite of my failures and weak-
   nesses
and to enrich my life.

Bind us close together in you
and enable us to help one another
on our earthly journey
so that we may be in heaven forever
with you and your Divine Son.

For Help in Trials

Have pity on me,
Mother of my Savior,
and grant me consolation in my trials.
Plead my cause before the Lord
and keep me from further worry and pain.
Ask God to pardon me for all my sins;
may your merits and prayers atone for them.
In you are salvation and life,
unending joy and a glorious eternity.

Invocations to Mary

O Mary, conceived without sin,
pray for us who have recourse to you.

*   *   *

Remember, O Virgin Mother of God,
as you stand in the sight of the Lord,
to speak for us, your little children.

*   *   *

Pray for us, O Holy Mother of God,
that we may be worthy of the promises of
    Christ.

For Mary's Protection Every Day

Holy Mother Mary,
I place myself under your loving protection
and ask the help of your intercession.
Immaculate Mary, Morning Star, Star of the
    Sea,
light the way for me.
May I be cheerful and pleasant to others this
    day
and especially to those in my own home.

For Preservation from Sin

O Mother of God,
Mary most holy,
how many times I have sinned.
But you, in your kind mercy, have rescued me.

Help me to overcome the hardness of my heart;
gently draw me to place all my trust in you.
Loving Mother,
preserve me from sin by your graces.

O my Queen, I am grateful
for all your many mercies and blessings.
I love you, next to God, above all things.
Permit not that I ever turn my back on you.
Through your intercession
keep me close to your Divine Son on earth,
that I may rejoice with you forever in heaven.

For My Relatives

Mary, my Mother,
pray for all my relatives.
Grant them health of mind and body.
Make them love God with all their hearts
and practice only those things
that are pleasing to Him.
Keep them safe from all harm
and bring them to your Son's eternal home
after their earthly pilgrimage.

For the Sick and the Dying

O Mother of help,
please assist the sick and the dying.
Give your special love to those who die this
day.
Help all the poor souls in purgatory.
Assist all who are in need,

especially those who are hungry in soul and
  body.
What comfort you bring us!
We are most grateful,
dear Mother.

In Sickness

Holy Mary, Mother of God,
and my Mother,
I come before you
in the knowledge that you will help me.
My faith tells me so
and my heart makes me sure of this.
In my sickness,
and in the midst of my suffering,
I often call out to you: "Mother!"
Just saying this word
makes me feel better.

When I feel misunderstood and all alone,
I know that you are with me
and that you love me.
Help me, Mary,
and when I am well let me love God more.

For the Souls in Purgatory

Jesus, Mary, and Joseph,
give eternal rest to the poor souls.
Jesus, Mary, and Joseph,
let perpetual light shine upon them.
May they rest in peace.

For Spiritual Strength

Holy Virgin Mary,
Mother of Jesus and my Mother,
keep me free from sin
and protect me in all dangers of soul and
  body.
Help me today in my work.
Make me faithful to you
so that I may give glory to God
and save my soul.

For a Good Spouse

Mary Immaculate,
sweet Mother of the young,
I entrust to your special care the decision
that I am to make as to my future husband
  (wife).
You are my Guiding Star!
Direct me to the person
with whom I can best cooperate
in doing God's holy Will
and with whom I can
live in peace, love, and harmony in this life
and attain to eternal joys in the next.

In Time of Sorrow

Mother of God,
look down upon a poor sinner
who has recourse to you.
Dear Mother,
I put my trust in you.

You stood beneath the Cross
and saw your Son die for us sinners
because He wished so much to save us.
O good Mother,
O Mother of mercy,
have pity on us,
your little children.

In Time of Worry

Dear Blessed Mother,
many times I worry and am anxious.
Please take these worries from me,
so that, at peace, I may help others
and think less about myself.
You are the advocate of the most miserable
    and abandoned;
you are the special friend of sinners.

Help me.
Come to my assistance.
I commend myself to you
and place in your hands all who are in need.

To Be Truly Human

Dear Mother Mary,
your Divine Son embraced our humanity
and so taught us how to be truly human.
Help me to follow His example
and bring out in myself all that is truly human.

Teach me to appreciate the immense good
that lies in being human,
climaxed by the gift of genuine self-giving.

Enable me to make use of all the gifts God
  has given me
in the way He desires they be used,
especially for the good of others.
Make me realize that only when I am
  genuinely human
can I be a true follower of your Divine Son.

To Know My Vocation

Dear Mother Mary,
God selected you to be the Mother of His
  Son
and to have a definite vocation,
and you freely consented to it
for your good
and the good of the human race.
Make me realize that each of us also has a
  vocation,
some state in life that God intends for us
for our own good
and the good of the whole human race.

Help me to know my vocation
and to follow it with joy and dedication.
Never let me lose hope,
for God has given me the talents
to succeed in any state to which He calls
  me.

To Know God's Will

Dearest Mother,
help me to remember
that I am made in the image and likeness of
    God.
Grant that all the thoughts of my mind,
all the words of my tongue,
all the affections of my heart,
and all the actions of my being
may always be conformed to the Divine Will.

Between me and God's most distant desire
let there be no veil that you have not removed,
no barrier that you have not torn down,
no infection that you have not cured,
no door that you have left unopened,
so that you may place my heart
within the radiance of God's knowledge
and make me taste the fragrance of His love.

For a Woman in Childbirth

Hail, O Queen of Heaven,
Mother of Mercy,
Consolation of Life,
and Joy of those who love you!
We cry out to you
on behalf of this poor sufferer.

In your Motherly goodness,
take pity on her.
Do not abandon her in her pains,
since she places a childlike confidence in you.

Through your own blessed delivery
and your Divine Son,
stand by her and gladden her with a happy
   delivery,
that she may gratefully praise your kindness.

In all our troubles and necessities,
we fly to you for help,
O Blessed Virgin Mary.

For World Peace

Dearest Mother,
with all my heart I honor you.
Bless me and guard me,
guide me and keep me.
You are my consolation and my comfort.
Blessed are you.
Break down the walls
of hatred and prejudice in the world
and bring peace for all human beings.

Mother of God,
I sing your praise.
Inspire me to love your Son more.

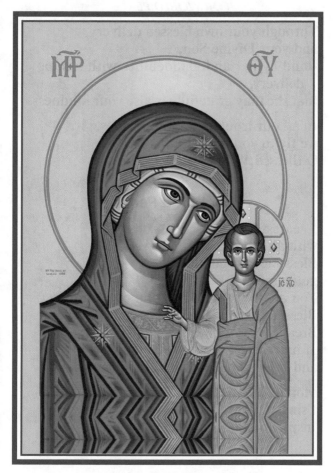

MARY AND THE CHURCH YEAR—From the moment of His Birth Mary was united with her Son in His redemptive work. As we celebrate the annual liturgical cycle of Christ's Mysteries, we honor Mary with special love, and on her feasts we pray to her with particular devotion.

PRAYERS FOR THE
LITURGICAL SEASONS

Each year, the Church helps us to meditate on the totality of the Christian Mystery through the medium of the Liturgical Year. She also desires that our prayer-life should proceed in accord with the major themes of that year. Hence, prayers to Mary could follow a pattern such as the following.

During Advent, we pray with the Immaculate Virgin in expectation of the coming of her Son.

During Christmas Time, we venerate Mary as the Mother of Christ and the servant of the Lord.

During Lent, we hail Mary as the collaborator with God and the witness of Christ's Passion.

During Easter Time, we see Mary as the first among the redeemed, the first believer, and the witness of the power of the Spirit,

During Ordinary Time, Mary is always before us in our growth in faith—in the Ordinary of the Mass but also in her feasts that occur throughout this time. She is there as the Mother showing continual interest in her children (Our Lady of Lourdes, Feb. 11), as the praying Virgin teaching us how to ponder God's Word in our hearts (Immaculate Heart of Mary, 3rd Saturday after Pentecost), as the garden-paradise leading us to Christ (Our Lady of Mount Carmel, July 16), and as the temple of God and the new Jerusalem calling us home (Dedication of St. Mary Major, Aug. 5).

Mary is with us as the image and the commanding proof of the fulfillment of our final hope (Assumption, Aug. 15) and as the Queen and Intercessor sitting beside the King of Ages (Queenship of Mary, Aug. 22). She is with us as the hope of the world and the dawn of salvation (Birth of Mary, Sept. 8) and as the suffering Mother (Our Lady of Sorrows, Sept. 15).

Mary is with us in the victories of the History of Salvation (Our Lady of the Rosary, Oct. 7) and as the exemplar of dedication to God (Presentation of Mary, Nov. 21).

Accordingly, this section offers prayers for each liturgical Season and each Feast of Mary to help us get into the habit of praying to Mary in accord with the Year of the Church. In doing so, we will be praying with the mind of the Church and in perfect harmony with Christ in His Mysteries.

Prayers for the Liturgical Seasons

ADVENT

For Christ's Triple Coming

Immaculate Virgin Mary,
your Son once came to rid the world of sin;
may He come to cleanse me of every sin.
Dearest Mother,
Jesus once came to save what was lost;
may He now come again with His saving power
so that those He redeemed will not be punished.
Dearest Mother,
I have come to know your Son in faith;
may I have unending joy when He comes again
in glory.

For Christ's Coming in Grace

Immaculate Virgin Mary,
during this Advent may Jesus come to us in
grace.
May He come to prepare our hearts, minds,
and bodies
to welcome Him on Christmas day.
May He come to comfort us in sadness,
to cheer us in loneliness,
to refresh us in weariness,
to buttress us in temptations,
to lead us in doubt,
and to exult with us in joy.

CHRISTMAS TIME

For Christ's Rebirth in the Church

Virgin Mother of Christ,
we do not ask that Jesus renew for us
His birth according to the flesh.
We ask that He incarnate us
in His invisible Divinity.
May He accomplish now in His Church
what He accomplished corporally in you.
May the Church's sure faith conceive Jesus,
her unstained intelligence give birth to Him,
and her soul united with the power of the
   Most High
preserve Him forever.

For Christ to Be Known to All

Virgin Mother of Christ,
obtain for us a new Epiphany
when your Son will be manifested to the world:
to those who do not know Him,
to those who do not want Him,
to those who vilify His Name,
to those who oppress His Mystical Body,
to those who deny Him,
and to those who unconsciously long for Him.

Bring the day closer
when all people will know and love Him
with the Father and the Holy Spirit
together with you—
and the Kingdom of God will have arrived.

LENT

To Be Freed of the Seven Deadly Sins

O Queen of Peace,
implant in me the virtues of gentleness and
  patience.
Let me curb the fury of *anger*
and restrain all resentment and impatience
so as to overcome evil with good,
attain your Son's peace,
and rejoice in His love.

O Model of Humility,
divest me of all *pride* and *arrogance.*
Let me acknowledge my weakness and sin-
  fulness,
so that I may bear mockery and contempt
for the sake of Jesus
and esteem myself as lowly in His sight.

O Teacher of Abstinence,
help me to serve you rather than my appetites.
Keep me from *gluttony*—
the inordinate love of food and drink—
and let me hunger and thirst for God's justice.

O Lover of Purity,
remove all *lust* from my heart,
so that I may serve you with a pure mind
and a chaste body.

O Mother of the Poor,
help me to avoid all *covetousness* for earthly
  goods

and give me a love for heavenly things.
Inspire me to give to the needy,
just as your Son gave His life
that I might inherit eternal treasures.

O Exemplar of Love,
keep me from all *envy* and ill-will.
Let the grace of God's love dwell in me
that I may rejoice in the happiness of others
and bewail their adversities.

O zealous Mother of Souls,
keep me from all *sloth* of mind or body,
so that I may do all things
for and in you and your Divine Son Jesus.

To Follow Christ

Mary, Perfect Disciple of Christ,
your Divine Son was gentle and humble of
  heart,
full of compassion and maker of peace.
He lived in poverty
and suffered persecution for the cause of justice.
He chose the Cross as the path of glory
to show us the way of salvation.
Intercede on my behalf
that I may receive the Word of the Gospel
  joyfully
and live by His example,
as an heir and citizen of His Kingdom.

EASTER TIME

For True Faith in Christ

Mary, the First Believer,
on Easter morn,
Jesus rose from the tomb
and appeared to you.
You saw His glorified Body,
touched Him, and worshiped Him.
Help me to believe with all my heart
that Jesus is risen,
that He is reigning
with His glorified Body
and with His Divinity
for all eternity.
Then when my life is ended let me
be united with both of you
in the glory of heaven.

For the Easter Virtues

Mary, the First among the Redeemed,
the Resurrection of Christ your Son
has given me new life and renewed hope.
Help me to live as a new person
in pursuit of the Easter ideal.
Grant me the wisdom to know what I must do,
the will to want to do it
the courage to undertake it,
the perseverance to continue to do it,
and the strength to complete it.

ORDINARY TIME

For a Productive Faith

Mary, Woman of Faith,
increase my faith
and let it bear fruit in my life.
Let it bind me fast to other Christians
in the common certitude
that our Master is the God-Man,
your Divine Son Jesus,
Who gave His life for all.

Let me listen in faith
to the Divine Word that challenges me.
Help me to strive wholeheartedly
under the promptings of my faith
in the building of a world ruled by love.
Enable me to walk in faith
toward the indescribable future
that your Son has promised
to all who possess a productive faith in Him

Growing with the Church Year

Mary, Mother of the Church,
I know that all human relations take time
if they are to grow and deepen.
This is also true of my relations
with your Son Jesus, the Father, and the Spirit,
which must grow over the course of my life.
However, this growth is not automatic;
time alone means nothing
unless I add my earnest efforts to it.

Your Divine Son has inspired the Church
to set aside special times
when this growth can develop more intensely—
the special seasons of the Church Year.
Help me to take them seriously
and make a real attempt to use them well,
so that I will grow into the person
that Jesus wants me to be.

Making Use of Frequent Prayer

Mary, Model of Prayer,
let me realize that, like all prayer,
prayer of petition is primarily
a means of encountering God—
the Father, the Son, and the Holy Spirit—
and being sustained by God.
It is also a means of encountering you,
and asking you to intercede with God for us,
for you are the Mother of God's Son
and His most perfect disciple.
It is true that God knows our needs,
but He wants us to express our requests
to Him directly or through you.

Let me pray always
so that I will purify my intentions
and bring them into accord with God's Will.
Let me pray with fixed formulas
as well as in my own words.
I will then come to know and love you more
and in so doing know and love Jesus even
    more.

Feasts of Mary

January 1 — Holy Mother of God

Mary, Mother of God,
on this first day of the year,
we acclaim your grandeur.
Hail, Mother of the God-Man.
Hail, Mother most holy.
Hail, Mother of love and mercy.
Hail, Mother filled with kindness.
Hail, Mother of unending life.
We have a Father in God
and a Mother in you.

Most loving Mother,
watch over me every day
and at every moment.

February 2 — Presentation of the Lord

Mary, Virgin most obedient,
you submitted to the ceremony of the presentation
and made the offering demanded of the poor.
You gave us an example of perfect obedience
  to God's Law
and zeal for the edification of others.
You were the first to offer
to the Eternal Father
His Divine Son as the Victim for the world's
  Redemption.

After your example,
I wish to offer myself as a sacrifice to God
in union with Jesus.
Help me to abstain from those many hurtful
    things
that prevent the union of my soul
with God.

February 11 — Our Lady of Lourdes

Immaculate Mary,
you appeared to St. Bernadette
and gave her a mission to build up Lourdes
as a sacred shrine to bring people to God.
Through your intercession,
countless graces have been given
to the thousands of people
who have flocked to Lourdes.
Some have even received the grace of physical
    healing.

I join my prayers to the pilgrims at your shrine
who sing thousands of *Aves* to you.
I place all my trust in you
and give you all my love.

March 25 — Annunciation of the Lord

Mary, Handmaid of the Lord,
the Angel of the Lord announced to you
 that you were to be the Mother of Jesus.
You immediately accepted God's will and said:
"I am the handmaid of the Lord.
Let it be done to me as you say."

And the Son of God became Man in your
   womb.

Mary,
you are full of grace.
Watch over the grace I received at my Baptism.
Do not let me lose it
and let it grow day by day.
Help me always to say "Yes" to God's will
and so be worthy to receive the reward
that your Divine Son has in store for me.

May 31 — The Visitation

Mary, Virgin most charitable,
your love is strikingly shown forth in the Visitation,
Though you were the Mother of the Most High,
you wanted to become the nurse of Elizabeth
and the infant John.
Though you were declared blessed among
   women,
you considered yourself the servant
of two of God's beloved children.

Help me to return unceasing thanks to God
for His many favors.
Keep me humble in possessing and using them.
May I be found worthy
of your frequent visits with Jesus
to my heart in this life
and of the invitation to come and live
with you both for all eternity in heaven.

3rd Saturday after Pentecost
The Immaculate Heart of
the Blessed Virgin Mary

Mary, temple of God,
your Heart is the masterpiece of the Holy
   Trinity.
The Eternal Father unfolded His omnipotence
in order to form in you
a Heart full of sweetness and obedience to your
   Creator.
The Divine Son gave you a mother's Heart,
in which He wished to dwell
as in a sanctuary.
The Holy Spirit gave you
the Heart of a bride,
all burning with a love pure and ardent.

Your Heart is truly a mirror of all the virtues,
a vivid image and faithful copy
of the Sacred Heart of Jesus.
Keep me always in the love of your Heart,
that I may love you more
and be led to love Jesus
with my whole heart.

July 16 — Our Lady of Mount Carmel

Mary, Virgin most powerful,
I honor you under the title of Our Lady of
   Mount Carmel.
It recalls the hermits who remained in God's
   presence
night and day on Mount Carmel in Palestine.

Teach me also to stand always in God's presence
every moment of my life.
And to do so,
let me stay always in your presence,
calling upon your help.
Remember me in my needs,
and show yourself my Mother.

Shed upon me more and more the living light
of the flame that made you blessed.
Enkindle in me the heavenly love
with which you loved your dear Son Jesus.
Obtain for me from Jesus
the gifts of humility, chastity, and meekness,
which were the fairest adornments of your
immaculate soul.
And after my earthly pilgrimage,
grant that my soul may obtain the glory of
heaven
through the merits of Christ
and your intercession.

August 5 — Dedication of the Basilica of St. Mary Major

Mary most holy,
you are our Model
of perfect dedication to God.
Holiness is union with God through love.
Through love you consecrated yourself
with all your powers
to God,

the highest form of beauty and goodness.
You knew nothing but God and His love;
you wished for nothing but Him and His holy
Will;
you sought nothing but His greater honor.
I consecrate myself to you.

Teach me to understand that
personal consecration does not mean only
to place myself under your special protection,
but rather to live for God
in union with you
by avoiding every sin
and practicing every virtue.
Imitating you is the best way of imitating Jesus
and of obtaining your powerful protection.

August 15 — The Assumption

Mary, seated in glory,
after the completion of your earthly life,
you were assumed body and soul into heavenly
glory.
Jesus ascended into heaven
by His own power as Lord and Creator,
accompanied by Angels who paid Him homage.
You were taken to heaven by the power of God,
accompanied and upheld by Angels,
raised aloft by grace not by nature.

Your Assumption was not only the crowning of
a holy life for you,
but also a cause of joy and triumph for the
human race.

Together with the Ascension of Jesus,
your Assumption became for us
a sure pledge of resurrection and immortality.
Pray to Jesus for us your children
that we may resemble you in our exile
so that we may glorify Him in union with you
  forever.

August 22 — The Queenship of Mary

Mary, Queen of the Universe,
you are a Queen because you are the Mother of
  the Word Incarnate.
Christ is universal King because He rules all
  creatures
by His personal union with the Divinity.
He is King and you are Queen of all hearts.

Rule over us by the queenly power of your love
that the Kingdom of your Son—
the Kingdom of truth and life,
holiness and grace,
justice, love, and peace—
may come upon earth.
Grant grace to all people,
the Holy Spirit for the Church,
and peace for the whole world.

September 8 — The Nativity of the B.V.M.

Mary our hope,
I rejoice with the Blessed Trinity
on your birthday
because you were to take part

in the Incarnation and Redemption of the world.
I rejoice with all humankind
because you are our life.
You bore Jesus,
Who is the Way, the Truth, and the Life,
and Who was to restore to humankind
the supernatural life that had been lost.

I have every reason to rejoice,
for as the Mother of Jesus and my Mother
you are my hope of salvation.
Through your prayers,
may I learn to know and love you more
and ever remain your faithful child.
This is my sure way of reaching heaven and my
   God.

September 15 — Our Lady of Sorrows

Mary, Mother of Sorrows,
your power to suffer was great on earth.
You were associated in all that Jesus did,
His sufferings as well as His joys.
On Calvary, you saw Him crucified
and received His dead body into your arms.
What sorrow this constituted for your Mother's
   heart!
But we know that this suffering enabled you
to become the Mother of Life,
the Mother of supernatural life for souls.

You can now suffer no more,
but those who are left on earth still suffer.
Help me to offer all my sufferings and sorrows,

no matter how big or how little,
for the Church of God
and for the souls of all peoples.

October 7 — Our Lady of the Rosary

Mary, Queen of the Holy Rosary,
your Divine Son Jesus is the perfect Mediator
between God and human beings,
because He alone could in all justice merit
our reconciliation with God
as well as the graces that God would impart
after the reconciliation.
You are a Mediatrix in union with Christ
from Whom your mediation draws all its
    power.
You merited the title of Unique Associate
above all by your union with Christ
in His redemptive sacrifice.
After Jesus, no one suffered as you did.
Now your action is primarily one of interces-
    sion.
In your contemplation of God,
you behold our needs with our prayers
and you beg God to grant these favors.

May the faithful recitation of my Rosary
be a sign of my gratitude to Jesus and to you
for all you have done for me
in bringing about my Redemption.
May my Rosary also be a means
of obtaining all the graces I need
for the sanctification and salvation of my soul.

November 21 — Presentation of the Blessed Virgin Mary

Mary, Virgin most obedient,
already in your childhood
you dedicated yourself to the love and service
    of God.
Led by Divine inspiration to His house,
you prepared yourself for your sublime dignity
of Divine Motherhood
in silence and solitude with God.
You followed with devotion
the life led in common by other girls
under the care of holy women.
When you later returned home,
you were under the care of your mother, St.
    Anne.

May the perfect gift of yourself to God
through love in your presentation in the temple
be an inspiration to me.
Obtain for me the grace to love God
with my whole heart and mind and strength.
May I too consecrate myself to God
under your patronage,
assisted by your intercession,
and in union with your love and merits.

December 8 — Immaculate Conception of the Blessed Virgin Mary

Mary, Virgin most pure,
your greatness began
at the first instant of your existence

with the privilege of your Immaculate Conception.

It was fitting that you should be adorned
with the greatest purity ever possible to a creature.

You are the Immaculate Virgin to whom God the Father decreed
to give His only Son.

You are the Immaculate Virgin
whom God the Son Himself chose to make His Mother.

You are the Immaculate Virgin
whom the Holy Spirit willed to make His Bride
and in whom He would work the tremendous miracle
of the Incarnation.

Help me to imitate your sinlessness
by keeping my soul free from willful sin
through the faithful observance of God's commandments.

Let me imitate your fullness of grace
by frequent reception of Communion
and assiduous prayer—
which will make my soul holy
and give me the grace I need to practice virtue.
Transform me into a living image of Jesus,
just as you were.

December 12 — Our Lady of Guadalupe

Mary, Mother of the Americas,
your apparition at Guadalupe teaches me

that devotion to you is a source of great graces.
God has entrusted to your hands heavenly
    blessings.
I have but to ask for them
for the salvation of my soul.
There is nothing you want more
than to give them to me,
because you are even more anxious to save my
    soul
than I am,
for you know better than anyone else
the price your Son paid for it
and the precious worth of each grace
that He so graciously offers to me through you.

Let me turn to you
as a child turns to its mother in every need
and finds comfort in her glance and kind word.
For you are truly my Mother,
whose Heart is overflowing with kindness and
    mercy.

MARY IS QUEEN OF HEAVEN—After her glorious Assumption into heaven, Mary was crowned Queen by her Divine Son. As the Queen of all, she listens to the prayers of her servants sojourning on earth and intercedes with Jesus on our behalf.

PRAYERS
FOR EVERY DAY

Those who are deeply devoted to our Blessed Mother are not of a mind to wait for her feasts or special Marian celebrations before praying to her. They want to pray to Mary every day—and at any given moment. The author of the Imitation of Mary, *a Christian classic, puts this sentiment in words:*

"Let us be careful to profit by the opportunities we have of pleasing Mary. Nothing seems too humble when her service is at stake, for indeed nothing is unimportant when it comes to serving the Mother of God, the Queen of the World. . . . Let us carefully offer her each day the tribute of our praise and the homage of our hearts."

Accordingly, this section offers Marian prayers for each month of the year and each day of the week. These follow the traditional Church pattern of assigning a particular Mystery of Christ to each month as well as each day of the week. Insofar as possible, the prayers given are those that accord best with the liturgical orientation of each month and day of the week. This enables Mary's clients to meditate on the pertinent aspect of their faith as they pray to Mary day by day.

Hence, those who use these prayers will be completely in tune with the mind of the Church at any given moment. At the same time, they will get to know Mary in the various stages of her life with Jesus and her present state of glory in heaven. They will obtain a better idea of Mary's role in the Mystery of Redemption, which her Son accomplished for the whole world.

In so doing, Mary's clients will also follow the fervent recommendation of the Church issued through the lips of Pope Pius XI: "By persevering prayer let us make Mary our daily Mediatrix, our true Advocate. In this way, we may hope that she herself, assumed into heavenly glory, will be our Advocate before Divine Goodness and Mercy at the hour of our passing."

As a kind of supplement, we have also included a few "Daily Prayers"—prayers that can be used day after day.

Prayers for Each Month of the Year

January — Mother of God

O Virgin Mother of God,
most august Mother of the Church,
I commend the whole Church to you.

You bear the sweet name of "Help of Bishops";
keep the bishops in your care,
and be at their side and at the side
of the priests, religious, and laity
who offer them help in sustaining the diffi-
    cult work
of the pastoral office.
From the Cross,
the Divine Savior, your Son,
gave you as a most loving Mother
to the disciple whom He loved;
remember the Christian people who commit
    themselves to you.

Be mindful of all your children;
join to their prayers
your special power and authority with God.
Keep their faith whole and lasting,
strengthen their hope,
and enkindle their love.
Be mindful of those who find themselves
in hardship, in need, in danger
and especially those who are suffering perse-
    cution
and are kept in chains
because of their Christian faith.
Ask for strength of soul for them,
O Virgin Mother,
and hasten the longed-for day of their liber-
    ation.

Turn your eyes of mercy
toward our Separated Brethren,

and may it please you
that one day we be joined together once again—
you who gave birth to Christ,
the Bridge and the Artisan of unity
between God and human beings.
I commend the whole human race
to your Immaculate Heart,
O Virgin Mother of God.
Lead it to acknowledge Jesus
as the one true Savior.
Drive far from it
all the calamities provoked by sin.
Bring it peace,
which consists in truth, justice, liberty, and
   love.

February — Our Lady of the Presentation

Mary,
how pleasing to God is your offering
at the time of the Presentation of Jesus
in the Temple.
You offer the eternal Son of God,
clothed in the flesh He took from your virginal
   body.
Jesus is the Lamb of God
Who takes away the sins of the world.
He is the Beloved Son of God
in Whom the Father is well pleased.
There is nothing that you want more
than to see me perfectly dedicated to God
as Jesus and you were.

Help me to be faithful to my Baptismal
   Promises
by which I have renounced Satan
and pledged my loyalty to God.
Offer me like Jesus to God.
Make me more like the Victim Jesus,
that my whole life may be a living, holy sacrifice,
pleasing to God.
As you are the way by which God came to us,
so in the Divine Plan you are the way
by which we go back to God.
I abandon myself completely to your Motherly
   guidance,
that you may lead me to Jesus.

March — Our Lady of the Annunciation

Mary,
I venerate you as Our Lady of the Annunciation
and the Mother of the Redeemer.
You shared in the great work
of the Redemption of the world.
You gave the God-Man His body and blood,
by means of which He was to suffer and die
for the sins of the human race.
By your close union with Jesus in life,
you became His coworker
in sanctifying and saving souls.

I thank the Holy Spirit for working in you
the great miracle of the Incarnation of Jesus.

Through the same Spirit,
Jesus takes up His abode in me
in Holy Communion.
Jesus continues to dwell in me
by letting me share His Own Divine Life
through grace.
Make my heart glow with the same love
that filled your heart
when you adored the living presence of Jesus
within you.
Help me to imitate your humility, sinlessness,
    and love,
for which God chose you to be His Mother.

April — Our Lady of the Resurrection

Mary,
at the Resurrection of your Divine Son,
God's Anointed One,
your heart was filled with joy beyond all telling
and your faith was wonderfully exalted.
For it was in faith
that you conceived Jesus,
and it was in faith
that you awaited His Resurrection,
the strongest proof of His Divinity.
In the strength of faith
you waited for that day of light and life
when the night of death would be ended,
the whole world would exult,
and the infant Church would tremble with joy
at seeing again her immortal Lord.

You knew at that first Easter
that His Divine life was the model for our lives
and that He has merited for us
the grace of living for God.
Enable me to rise with Jesus spiritually
and live a life free from sin.
Help me to do God's Will
and to be patient in suffering.
Enrich my soul with sanctifying grace
through Sacraments, prayer, and good works.
And let the life of Jesus grow in me,
so that He may live in me.

May — Our Lady of the Trinity

Holiest Virgin,
with all my heart I venerate you
above all the Angels and Saints in heaven
as the daughter of the Eternal Father,
and I consecrate to you
my soul with all its powers.

Holiest Virgin,
with all my heart I venerate you
above all the Angels and Saints in heaven
as the Mother of the only-begotten Son,
and I consecrate to you
my body with all its senses.

Holiest Virgin,
with all my heart I venerate you
above all the Angels and Saints in heaven
as the beloved Spouse of the Holy Spirit,
and I consecrate to you
my heart with all its affections.

Holiest Virgin,
intercede for me with the Holy Trinity
that I may obtain the graces I need
for my salvation.
To you I entrust all my worries and miseries,
my life and the end of my life,
so that all my actions may be directed
by the Divine Plan.

June — Our Lady, Spouse of the Holy Spirit

Mary,
Mother of Jesus and my Mother,
I venerate you as the Immaculate Spouse
of the Holy Spirit.
You are the glory of Jerusalem,
the joy of Israel,
the honor of our nation.
As the valiant woman,
you crushed the head of the serpent
when you offered your Divine Son
to the heavenly Father
in the love of the Holy Spirit
for the salvation of the world.

Through the merits of this precious sacrifice
and through the sufferings of your Son,
obtain for me the gifts of the Holy Spirit.
I thank the Holy Spirit
for having chosen you as His Spouse
and made you the dispenser of His graces.
Look upon me with your compassionate eyes.
Behold my distress and my needs.

Help me never to lose the grace of God
or defile the temple of the Spirit,
that my heart may always remain His holy
  dwelling.
May I become His faithful child on earth,
as you were,
so that I may share His eternal glory in
  heaven.

July — Our Lady of Divine Providence

Mary,
Immaculate Virgin and Mother of Divine
  Providence,
keep my soul with the fullness of your grace.
Govern my life
and direct it in the way of virtue,
that I may fulfill the Divine Will.
Obtain for me
the pardon and remission of all my sins.
Be my refuge, my protection, my defense, and
  my guide
in my pilgrimage through the world.
Comfort me in the midst of trials.
Bring me safe through every danger.
Give me your sure protection in the storms of
  affliction.

Mary,
renew my heart spiritually,
that it may become a holy dwelling place
for your Divine Son Jesus.
Keep far from me every kind of sin,

negligence, carelessness, cowardice, and
  human respect.
You are the Mother of Providence
and the Virgin of pardon.
You are my hope on earth.
Grant that I may have you as my Mother
in the glory of heaven.

August — The Immaculate Heart
of Mary

Mary, Mother of God,
your Heart is a shrine of holiness
in which the demon of sin has never entered.
After the Heart of Jesus,
never was there a heart more pure and more
  holy.
Your Heart is a counterpart of the Heart of
  Jesus.
His Heart is a loving Heart.
Your Heart is also the most affectionate of
  hearts
after that of Jesus.
You love as a mother loves her children.
Your eyes ever watch over us;
your ears constantly listen to our cries;
your hands are always extended over us
to help us and impart heavenly gifts;
above all, your Heart is full of tenderest care
  for us.

The Heart of Jesus was a suffering Heart.
Your Heart was also a suffering heart.

Its martyrdom began with Simeon's prophecy in the Temple
and was completed on Calvary.

When the hands and feet of Jesus were pierced
with nails
the sound of each blow of the hammer
inflicted a wound in your Heart.
When His side was opened with a lance,
a sword of sorrow also pierced your Heart.

The Heart of Jesus was a pure Heart.
Your Heart was also a pure Heart,
free from the stain of original sin,
and from the least stain of actual sin.
Your Heart is pure and spotless
because it was sanctified beyond all other
hearts
by the indwelling of the Holy Spirit,
making it worthy to be the dwelling place
of the Sacred Heart of Jesus.

The Heart of Jesus was a generous Heart.
Your Heart is also a generous Heart,
full of love, abounding in mercy.
All people may find a place there as your
children
if only they choose to heed your loving appeal.
Your Heart is a refuge for sinners,
for you are the Mother of Mercy,
who have never been known to turn away
anyone who has come to seek your aid.

I consecrate myself entirely to your Immaculate Heart.
I give you my very being and my whole life:
all that I have,
all that I love,
all that I am.
I desire that all that is in me and around me
may belong to you
and may share in the benefits of your Motherly
blessing.

September — Our Lady Queen of Martyrs

Mary, most holy Virgin,
and Queen of Martyrs,
accept the sincere homage of my childlike love.
Welcome my poor soul
into your Heart pierced by so many sorrows.
Receive it as the companion of your sorrows
at the foot of the Cross,
on which Jesus died
for the Redemption of the world.

Sorrowful Virgin,
in union with you I will gladly suffer
all the trials, misunderstandings, and pains
that our Lord lets me endure.
I offer them all to you in memory of your sorrows,
so that every thought of my mind
and every beat of my heart
may be an act of compassion and love for you.

Loving Mother,
have pity on me
and reconcile me to your Divine Son.
Keep me in His grace
and assist me in my last agony,
so that I may be able to meet you in heaven
and sing your glories.

Mary most sorrowful,
Mother of Christians,
pray for us.
Mother of love, of sorrow, and of mercy,
pray for us.

October — Our Lady of the Rosary

Most holy Virgin,
you have revealed the treasures of graces
hidden in the recitation of the Rosary.
Inspire my heart with a sincere love
for this devotion,
so that by meditating on the Mysteries of our
   Redemption
that are recalled in it,
I may gather the fruits
and obtain the special graces I ask of you,
for the greater glory of God,
for your honor,
and for the good of my soul.

O Virgin Mary,
grant that the recitation of the Rosary
may be for me each day,
amid my manifold duties,

a bond of unity in my actions,
a tribute of filial piety,
a delightful refreshment,
and an encouragement to walk joyfully
along the path of my state in life.
Let the mysteries of your Rosary
form in me little by little
a luminous atmosphere,
pure, strengthening, and fragrant,
which may penetrate my understanding and
    will,
my heart and memory,
my imagination and my whole being,
so that I shall acquire the habit
of praying while I work.

November — Our Lady of Intercession

Mary,
Our Lady of Intercession,
your Motherly tenderness gathers in one em-
    brace
all the souls redeemed by the Precious Blood
of your Son Jesus.
I come before your royal throne
with sadness in my heart,
but also with boundless confidence in your in-
    tercession,
as I remember those who have gone before me.
Death, which tore apart the bonds of earth,
has not destroyed the love that binds me
to those who lived in the same faith as I do.

Mary,
countless souls in that place of expiation
await with inexpressible anxiety
the help of my prayers
and the merits of my good works.
Urged by the charity of Jesus,
I raise my face and heart in prayer to you,
on behalf of those Suffering Souls.
Grant that the burning desire of the Poor Souls
to be admitted to the Beatific Vision
may soon be satisfied.

I pray especially for the souls of my family
    members,
my friends and relatives,
those who were zealous in honoring you,
those who did good to others,
and those who are most forgotten.
Grant that we may all be united in heaven,
rejoicing in the possession of God,
and thanking you
for all the blessings you have obtained for us.

December — Mother of the Child Jesus

Mary,
how great was your love for Jesus.
Before His birth,
from the depths of your Heart
you sent your prayers to Him.
When the people's heartlessness thrust Jesus
    and you

from Bethlehem to the cold stable,
your arms warmed the Savior.
When Herod's cruelty drove you into the
   Egyptian desert,
your virginal breast was the only safe resting
   place
for your little Son.
When Jesus began to develop,
your pure eyes guarded Him day and night.
And when He struggled with death on Calvary,
it was you, His Mother,
who stood faithfully at the foot of the Cross
with the sword of pain piercing your Heart.

Like you,
help me to strive with every power within me
to love Jesus for His own sake.
May that love impress itself
on all my thoughts, words, and actions.
Like you,
let me willingly accept and bear the Cross
in the spirit of a true follower
of my crucified Master.
Your soul was stirred with sentiments of admi-
   ration
for the wondrous providence of God
when you saw the first adorers of your Divine
   Child
who had been led to the crib
by the message of the Angel.

Help me to learn the lesson of humility,
  poverty, and self-denial
that Jesus preached from His first pulpit, the
  little crib.

Prayers for Each Day
of the Week

Sunday — Our Lady of the Trinity

Our Lady of the Trinity,
Sunday is the Day of the Lord:
Father, Son, and Holy Spirit.
You are the beloved Daughter of the Father,
devoted Mother of the Son,
and exalted Bride of the Holy Spirit.
Help me to keep Sundays holy
by participating in the Eucharist
and dedicating myself to the things of God.

Grant that all the thoughts of my mind,
all the words of my mouth,
all the affections of my heart,
and all the actions of my life
may always be conformed to the Will of God.
Give me a great faith
to discern God here below,
in appearance and in a dark manner.
Then take me at last
to contemplate the ineffable Lord face to face
and to possess Him forever in heavenly glory
in union with you.

Monday — Our Lady of Grace

Our Lady of Grace,
Monday is the day of the Holy Spirit,
the Sanctifier.
Your soul was made full of grace
by the power of the Holy Spirit,
the third Person of the Trinity,
the uncreated love between the Father and the
    Son.
Through you I beg the merciful Father
to send the Holy Spirit of grace,
that He may bestow on me His sevenfold gifts.
May He send me the gift of *wisdom,*
which is none other than your Son Jesus;
the gift of *understanding,*
which will enlighten me;
the gift of *counsel,*
which will give me the strength to vanquish
the enemies of my sanctification and salvation.
May He impart to me the gift of *knowledge,*
which will enable me to discern
the teaching of your Son Jesus
and distinguish good from evil;
the gift of *piety,*
which will make me enjoy true peace;
and the gift of *fear of the Lord,*
which will make me shun all iniquity
and avoid all danger of offending
your Divine Son.

Pray for me,
O Lady of the Holy Spirit,

that I may be fruitful in good works
for the glory of God
and the spiritual and material good of all
   people.

Tuesday — Queen of the Angels and Saints

Queen of the Angels and Saints,
Tuesday is the day of the Angels.
Help me to realize that in praising the Angels
I praise God's glory,
for by honoring them
I honor their Creator,
Who saw fit to send His Angels
to watch over His servants on earth.
Grant that I may be always under their pro-
   tection
and one day enjoy their company in heaven.

Tuesday is also devoted to the Saints.
Enable me to see that God is glorified in them,
for their glory is the crowning of His gifts.
By their lives on earth,
He provides me with an example.
By my communion with them,
He gives me their friendship.
By their prayers,
He grants me strength and protection.
By this great company of witnesses,
He spurs me on to victory over evil
and the prize of eternal life.

Dear Mother Mary,
make me share the faith of the Saints on earth,
so that I may also experience their peace in
   heaven
together with you and your Divine Son.

Wednesday — Spouse of St. Joseph

Spouse of St. Joseph,
Wednesday is devoted to your husband,
the saintly carpenter who cared for you and
   Jesus
as part of the Holy Family.

In honor of this just man
who protected you and Jesus
from Herod who wanted to kill the Child,
save me from my many sins.
In honor of this foster father of Christ,
the Divine Physician,
sustain the sick and obtain relief for them.
In honor of this gentle man
who died in the arms of you and Jesus,
intercede for the dying.
In honor of this intrepid guardian
of the Holy Family,
protect all Christian families.
In honor of this dedicated and honest work-
   man,
teach me to labor for Jesus.
In honor of this faithful and chaste spouse,
preserve in my heart
a love of fidelity and purity.

Dear Mother Mary,
let me always revere St. Joseph
and imitate his life of total dedication
to you and Jesus.

Thursday — Our Lady of the Blessed Sacrament

Our Lady of the Blessed Sacrament,
Thursday is devoted to the Blessed Sacrament
in commemoration of the Last Supper
when Jesus left us the Holy Sacrifice of the
    Mass,
the memorial of His Passion, Death, and
    Resurrection.

My Mother Mary,
thank you for having given me the Eucharistic
    Christ
Who offers Himself to the Father
as the Victim of Calvary at every Mass,
Who gives Himself to me
as food in Holy Communion,
and Who abides with me in the tabernacle
as the best Friend I have in the world.
For this reason I honor you
as Our Lady of the Blessed Sacrament.
Make me a frequent apostle of the Eucharist
and so Eucharist-minded
that my very life may be the Eucharist.

Friday — Our Lady of Sorrows

Our Lady of Sorrows,
during your life on earth,
you were saddened many times
and specifically during the traditional Seven
   Sorrows:
the prophecy of Simeon at the presentation,
the flight into Egypt,
the three days' loss of Jesus,
the meeting with Jesus carrying His Cross,
His Death on Calvary,
His being taken down from the Cross,
and His burial in the tomb.
Your sorrow on Calvary was deeper
than any sorrow felt on earth,
for no mother in all the world
had a heart as tender as your Heart,
which was the Heart of the Mother of God.
You bore your sufferings for us
that we might enjoy the graces of Redemption.

Dear Mother Mary,
console me when I am sad,
and make me happy with your Motherly love.
Comfort me when I am in pain,
and heal the wounds of my spirit.
Fill my heart with your joy,
and make me forget the troubles of this life,
so that I may be happy forever
with you and your Divine Son in heaven.

Saturday — Our Lady, Queen of the World

Hail, O Mother, Queen of the world.
You are the Mother of Fair Love,
you are the Mother of Jesus,
and the source of all grace,
the fragrance of all virtue,
the mirror of all purity.
You are joy in weeping,
victory in the struggle,
and hope in death.

How sweet is your name in my mouth,
what delightful harmony in my ears,
what intoxication in my heart!
You are the happiness of the suffering,
the crown of martyrs,
and the beauty of virgins.

Queen of glory and honor,
keep my soul from all danger.
Take my humble prayers
and bring them to God's throne in heaven
that they may be answered.
May I honor you
on earth with all human beings
and in heaven with all the Saints and Angels.

Daily Prayers

Morning Prayer

O Mary, my Queen,
I cast myself in the arms of your mercy.
I place my soul and body
in your blessed care
and under your special protection
today and everyday
and above all at the hour of my departure
from this world.
I entrust to you all my hopes and consolations,
all my anguish and misery,
my life and the end of my life.
Through your most holy intercession
and through your merits,
grant that all my works may be directed and
    carried out
in accord with your will
and the will of your Divine Son.

St. Louis de Montfort

Evening Prayer

O Mary, my Mother,
by your Motherly prayers,
obtain pardon from Jesus
for the sins I have committed
this day—
in what I have done
and in what I have failed to do.

Help me to do better tomorrow
after a blessed rest
under your watchful eye.
If I should die before I wake,
please beg the Lord my soul to take.

Prayers during the Day

- Sweet Heart of Mary,
  be my salvation.
- Mary conceived without sin,
  pray for us who have recourse to you.
- O Mary,
  you entered the world without stain of sin;
  obtain for me from God
  that I may leave it without sin.
- Virgin most sorrowful,
  pray for us.
- Mother of love, of sorrow, and of mercy,
  pray for us.
- Holy Mary,
  make my heart and my body pure.
- Queen of the Most Holy Rosary,
  pray for us.
- Mother of Perpetual Help,
  pray for us.
- O Mary,
  help me to live in God,
  with God, and for God.
- O Virgin Mary,
  Mother of God,
  pray to Jesus for me.

Prayer before Communion

O Mary, my Mother,
you carried in your womb
the God Whom I am going to receive.
Help me by your powerful intercession
to receive Him with humility and love.
Prepare my heart through abundant grace
for the worthy reception
of the Body and Blood of Jesus.

On earth you were so steadfast in His love.
Invest me with your merits
and adorn me with your virtues.
Let me share in your good works,
that the Lord of Heaven may find me
richly endowed with merit
and pleasing in His eyes.

Prayer after Communion

Most holy Mother,
now that I have received Jesus
in His holy Sacrament of love,
unite my soul to His Soul
and my being to His Being.
You gave the form to your Infant God
when He took our human nature;
make me over
according to the likeness of your Son.

Place my poor weak heart in His Heart,
that it may be filled with His sentiments
and His charity.

Let me think as Jesus thought
and let me always act in word and deed
as He did—
in humility, simplicity, and love.
Obtain the same for all those
to whom I am united by any bonds, human or
    Divine,
that all of us may become pleasing
in your sight
and the sight of God.

INDEX OF PRAYER THEMES
(Bold type indicates eight divisions of the book)